best music coach

MW01231172

1

MUSIC THEORY WORKBOOK

The Fast and Easy Way to "Get" Music Theory
For Beginners

MUSIC THEORY WORKBOOK 1
IS NOT A TEXTBOOK
USE IT WITH
THE BEST MUSIC THEORY BOOK FOR BEGINNERS: 1
to learn about music theory

Welcome to Best Music Coach!

A note to adult students and parents of younger students

I am so glad that you chose this book to assist you on your journey to becoming a more well rounded musician. As a peer tutor for two years at the world-renowned Berklee College of Music, I taught concepts ranging from music theory (classical and jazz), to arranging, to composition, to ear training all the way to counterpoint. I tutored students from every continent, from dozens of countries and musical backgrounds.

In this book, in collaboration with Lead Coach Dan Spencer, I aimed to present the most fundamental music theory concepts in the best possible way for building knowledge and becoming a more well-rounded musician. Together, we put a great amount of thought into the best way to present the material and the order of its presentation with the end result of diverse musical competencies in mind. All of the exercises in this book (and continuing into future levels) will be directly applied to making music - through performance, composition, and/or imagination.

It is important to note that the term "music theory" in this book refers to the system which comes from Western European classical music. It is by no means the only method to understand, analyze, and learn music, nor is it necessarily the best. There are other systems of music theory, especially those which are based more heavily on aural recognition and comprehension, that can benefit a musician in ways that the Western European classical method does not. Conversely, there are ways in which the Western European method can benefit musicians in ways that other music learning methods cannot.

As a professional composer of music, I want to emphasize that the Western European classical method, which this book is based on, has played a fundamental role in not only my career as a musician, but that of countless others too. I see the various methods of learning music like tools in a toolkit, where the Western European classical method is like a Swiss army knife, as it is versatile in many situations. It can help you as a performer, improviser, composer, educator, arranger, orchestrator, music editor, and beyond.

My hope is that you will take the knowledge from this book and future books to help you achieve your musical dreams.

- Eli Slavkin
Coach

Contents

How to Scan QR Codes

1

2

3

1. On an iPhone open the camera. On Android, download and open a QR code scanner application.

2. Hold your phone so you can see the QR code on the screen, and the screen is in focus.

3. On iPhones, tap the banner that asks you if you want to open the QR code. On Android, tap the button that asks you to open the QR code.

Open QR code?

Music Theory: Introduction

What is Music Theory?

The study and understanding of the elements and structure of music. To put it simply, music theory is the key to understanding the "how" and the "why" behind the music you hear or play.

Why Learn Music Theory?

Learn Pieces of Music Faster on any Instrument or Voice

Just like using a map or GPS app will help you get to your destination faster, music theory can act as the map or GPS app to show you the way to the end of a piece of music, speeding memorization and in some cases increasing your emotional connection to the music built on understanding what is actually going on.

Get Better at Reading Music

Understanding all the intricacies of music theory will improve your ability to read music. Many things you will learn in this book will give you a stronger relationship to written music.

Strengthen Your Relationship to All the Music in your Life

Music theory will help you understand and relate to the music you are hearing, singing and/or playing. With this understanding, you will be able to play the music more accurately, with a deeper intellectual and emotional understanding and interpretation. Think about how many new things you have learned so far in your life from reading books. How much more could you learn about music from being able to read and understand what is happening in a piece of music? Music theory will make you a smarter and sharper musician when playing, writing, and studying music.

What You Will Need

1. This book.
2. *The Best Music Theory Book for Beginners 1*
3. Manuscript paper.
4. Pencils.
5. A ruler.

Scan the code below for our recommendations.

How This Book Works

How to Understand Exercises

You may find exercises and ideas easier to understand with a music teacher or coach. If you have not read "The Best Music Theory Book for Beginners 1" you may not understand the exercises and ideas in this book. Buy a 3rd edition copy if you have not already.

FREE Answer Keys

Download your FREE copy of the answer keys for this entire book by scanning the QR code below or at https://bestmusiccoach.com/courses/music-theory-workbook-1

FREE Online Quiz and Certificate

When you complete the final quiz for this book with 95% correct answers, you will receive an official full-color certificate of achievement that you can print out, download, share on social media and keep forever as a sign of your accomplishments in music theory.

Scan the QR code below to go to: https://bestmusiccoach.com/courses/music-theory-workbook-1

Workbook

Rhythm 1: How to Understand, Write, and Perform Notes

Staff Line and Space ID

Line 5
Line 4
Line 3
Line 2
Line 1

Space 4
Space 3
Space 2
Space 1

Identify the line or space that the dot (notehead) is placed on. Write in the blank below each dot L for line and S for space followed by the number of the line or space.

Example

S1 L3 S3 L4   S3 L5 L2 S3   L3 L5 L3 L1   S4 L3 S2 L1

Exercise 1

Write S and the number space the dot (notehead) is in.

___ ___ ___ ___ ___ ___ ___ ___ ___ ___ ___ ___ ___ ___ ___ ___

Exercise 2

Write L and the number space the dot (notehead) is in.

___ ___ ___ ___ ___ ___ ___ ___ ___ ___ ___ ___ ___ ___ ___ ___

Exercise 3

A mix of lines and spaces.

___ ___ ___ ___ ___ ___ ___ ___ ___ ___ ___ ___ ___ ___ ___ ___

Writing Noteheads

Closed Noteheads

Closed noteheads should be written as a tilted oval.

Open Noteheads: Half Notes

Open noteheads for half notes should also be written with a tiled oval shape.

Open Noteheads: Whole Notes

Open noteheads for whole notes should be oval and not tilted.

Alternate between tracing and writing the three types of noteheads. Color in and trace the gray noteheads, then try to copy them free hand in the bank spaces. Review p. 15 of *The Best Music Theory Book for Beginners* before beginning.

Example

Exercise 1: Closed Noteheads

Exercise 2: Open Noteheads: Half Notes

Exercise 3: Open Noteheads: Whole Notes

Exercise 4: Open Noteheads: Whole Notes

Exercise 5: Mix

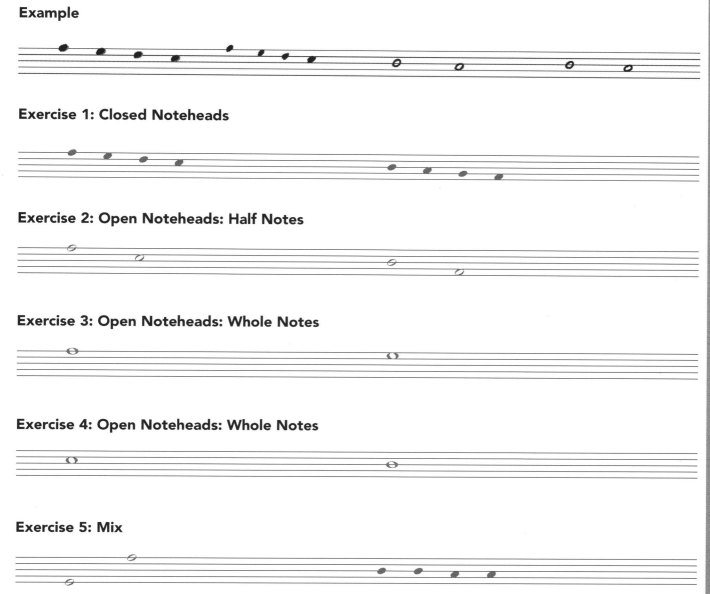

Writing Stems

In the following exercises, you will practice writing stems with the correct length on each notehead. Remember to pay careful attention to the direction of the stem (up or down). See the examples below.

Stem Direction: Stem Down

On or above line 3 of the staff

Stem Direction: Stem Up

Below line 3 of the staff

Example

Add the correct stem (length and direction) for each notehead.

Answer

Remember that the length of each stem should be the lengths of four lines of the staff.

Exercise 1

Add the correct stem (length and direction) for each quarter notehead. Remember that all notes which are under the middle line of the staff should have their stem pointing upwards. All notes above and on the middle line have their stems pointing downwards.

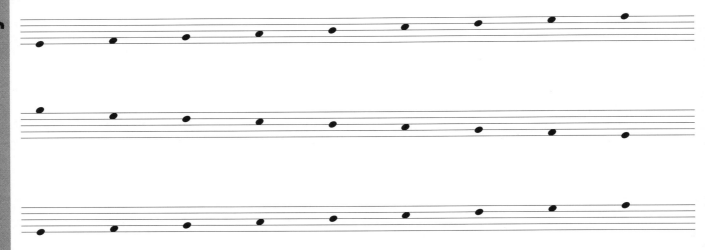

Exercise 2

Add the correct stem (length and direction) for each half notehead.

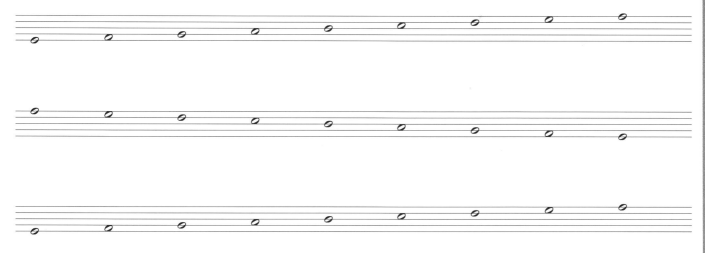

Exercise 3

Add the correct stem (length and direction) for each quarter notehead. This time, pay close attention to the direction of the stem, since the notes are in a random order.

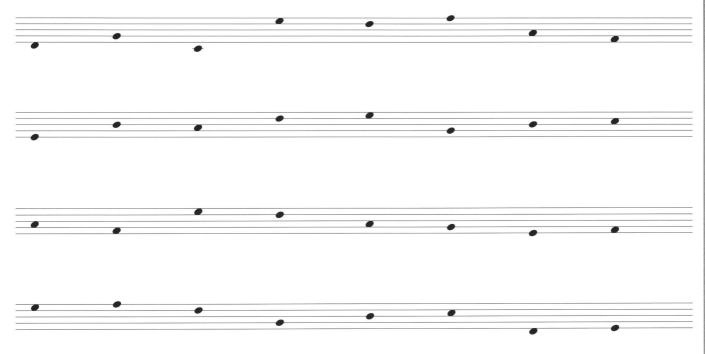

Mini quiz 1:

1. Noteheads which are above the middle line of the staff should point _____

2. When a notehead is on the middle line, it usually should point _____

Note Tracing Exercises

In this exercise, trace the notehead and the stem facing up for each note. Remember, the noteheads should be tilted ovals which touch the line or space both directly above & directly below each note. Stems extend 4 lines of the staff. Since this exercise only includes below line 3 of the staff, this means the stems should be facing upwards.

Remember to leave the notehead empty for half notes!

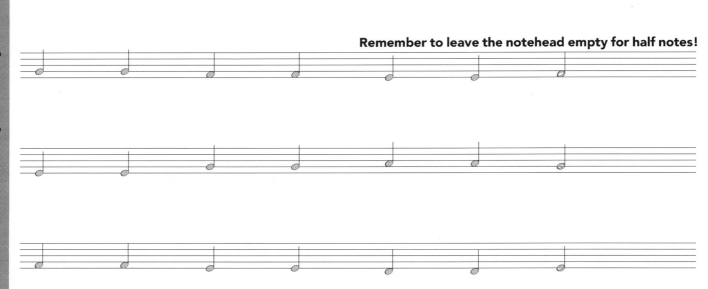

In this next exercise, trace the notehead and stem facing down for each note. Since exercise 2 only includes notes above line 3 of the staff, this means the stems should face down.

Writing Bar Lines

There are many different types of bar lines in music, which are used not only to separate measures, but also to separate different parts of a song.

Reminder: The three most common types of bar lines are:

1. Regular Bar Line (these are used to separate measures).

2. Double Bar Line (these are used often to separate sections or show the end of an exercise that does not happen in regular measures).

3. End Bar Line (these are used to end the song).

Exercise 1

Copy the bar lines from the top staff by writing them onto the bottom staff.

Exercise 2

Copy the double bar lines from the top staff by writing them onto the bottom staff.

Exercise 3

Copy the final bar lines from the top staff by writing them onto the bottom staff.

Writing Time Signatures

The time signature is an important part of written sheet music. In these exercises, you will practice writing your own time signatures.

Remember: The two time signatures which you have learned so far are  and . Remember that in order to write the time signature, you place two large numbers on top of each other.

The **upper number** of the time signature takes up the space from line 3 to line 5 of the staff

The **lower number** of the time signature takes up the space from line 1 to line 3 of the staff.

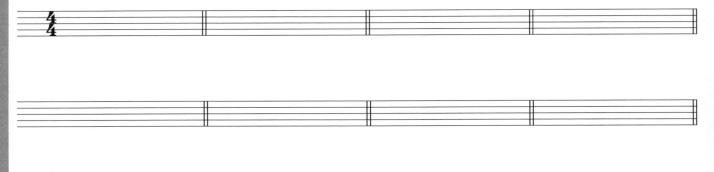

Exercise 1

In each blank measure, write the time signature for $\frac{4}{4}$. Leave some open space to the left of each time signature, between the time signature and the double bar line.

Exercise 2

In each blank measure, write the time signature for $\frac{3}{4}$. Leave some open space to the left of each time signature.

Writing Percussion Clefs

To write a percussion clef:

    1. Write two vertical lines from the 4th line of the staff to the 2nd line of the staff.

    2. Make the lines thick.

Exercise

Using the above steps, fill in the following 12 measures with percussion clefs. The first measure of each line is already filled in for you.

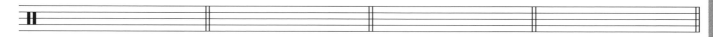

The other name for a percussion clef is "neutral clef".

Writing Percussion Clefs and Time Signatures

    1. Write a percussion clef then the indicated time signature in every measure. The first measure of both exercises is completed as an example.

4/4 Exercise

3/4 Exercise

Writing Lines of Music 1

1. Write a barline in the middle of the line of staff.

2. Write two more bar lines on either side of the first bar line.

3. Write a percussion clef, time signature, and final bar line.

Example

Exercise 1

Write a percussion clef, time signature for $\frac{4}{4}$ then write the barlines and final barline on each line of blank staff.

Exercise 2

Write a percussion clef, time signature for $\frac{3}{4}$ then write the barlines and final barline on each line of blank staff.

Spacing Notes on the Staff

In the following exercises, you will write your own notes (both the notehead and stem). The goal of these exercises is to pay close attention to the proper spacing between each note.

Spacing Notes on the Staff: 𝄴

In this exercise, write the noteheads on space 2 of the staff above each number. The numbers represent which beat of the measure the note will start on after you write it. Look to the next number to see how long the note will last (rhythmic duration) to see if the note you should write is a whole, half, or quarter note. Pay attention to the spacing and how many beats (4) should be in each measure.

Exercise 1

1   2   3   4   1   3

Answer 1

The measure below has one note on beat 1, and another on beat 3. Remember, it takes two half notes to fill one measure of 𝄴, since each half note lasts for two beats.

1   2   3   4   1   3

Exercise 2

1   2   4   1

Answer 2

In the measure below the half note is on beat 2, and lasts for two beats. Leave space before adding the quarter note on beat 4.

Which note takes up one whole measure of 𝄴? A whole note!

1   2   4   1

1. There are no hints or answer keys for these next exercises. Use what you have learned.

2. Add a time signature and percussion clef.

3. Write all noteheads on line 3 of the staff with stem down for half and quarter notes.

Exercise 3

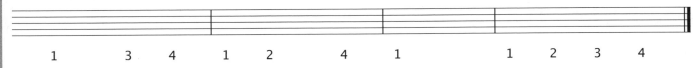

1   3   4   1   2   4   1   1   2   3   4

Exercise 4

1   2   3   1   1   2   3   4   1   3

Exercise 5

1   2   4   1   2   3   4   1   2   3   1   3   4

Exercise 6

1   1   3   1   1   2   4

Exercise 7

1   2   3   1   3   1   1   2   4

Exercise 8

1   2   3   4   1   1   3   4   1   2   3   4

Whole notes fill up an entire measure of $\frac{4}{4}$. But what type of note fills up a measure of $\frac{3}{4}$? Answer: a dotted half note! You will learn about these cool, new notes in a later chapter.

Spacing Notes on the Staff: $\frac{3}{4}$

Remember that the $\frac{3}{4}$ time signature has 3 beats per measure. This is because the top note in a time signature always refers to the number of beats in the measure.

Exercise 1

1   3   1   2   3   1   3   1   2

Answer

1   3   1   2   3   1   3   1   2

1. Add a time signature and percussion clef.

2. Write all noteheads on line 3 of the staff with stem down for half and quarter notes.

Exercise 2

1   3   1   2   1   2   3   1   3

Exercise 3

1   2   3   1   3   1   3   1   2

Exercise 4

1   2   1   2   3   1   3   1   3

Exercise 5

1   3   1   3   1   2   1   2   3

Review: Rhythm 1

- Rhythm
- Pulse

Pulse: sound
Pulse: feeling

- Beat
- The metronome
- Count in
- Tempo/Time
- Lines

Single line
Staff (five lines)

- Notes

Whole Notes
Half Notes
Quarter Notes

- The staff: lines and spaces
- How to write noteheads

Closed noteheads
Open noteheads: half notes
Open noteheads: whole notes
In a space
On a line

- How to write stems

Stem down notes: p
Stem up notes: d
Stem length
Stem direction

- How to write whole, half, and quarter notes
- How to clap notes

Quarter notes
Half notes
Whole notes
Why we clap
How to clap fast

- Bar lines and their meanings

Regular bar line
Double bar line
Final bar line

New Words You Should Know

1. Rhythm
2. Pulse
3. Beat
4. Metronome
5. Tempo
6. Staff
7. Notehead
8. Stem
9. Bar line
10. Measure
11. Attack
12. Time signature
13. Clef

- Measures

m. = measure
mm. = measures

- What is an "attack" in music?
- Composer vs. songwriter
- Time signatures

When a note get the beat it gets the count

- Percussion clef
- How to write music 1

Measure math

How to write lines of music

How to write whole notes, half notes, and quarter notes in a measure

How to write and perform your own compositions

Workbook
Rhythm 2: Strong and Weak Beats 1

Strong and Weak Beats

It might not seem important now, but the strong and weak beats are REALLY important for when you start to understand and break down your favorite songs and understand music.

Strong and Weak Beats in $\frac{4}{4}$

Write the order of strong and weak beats!

Strongest _____ _____ Weakest

_____ _____ Strong _____

_____ _____ _____ _____

Strong and Weak Beats in $\frac{3}{4}$

Write the order of song and weak beats!

_____ _____ Weakest

_____ Weak _____

Strongest _____ _____

_____ _____ _____

Review: Rhythm 2

- Strong and weak beat culture
- Strong and weak beat colors

 Strongest

 Strong

 Weak

 Weakest

New Words You Should Know

1. Music culture
2. Snare
3. Kick

- Strong and weak beats in $\frac{4}{4}$

- Strong and weak beats in $\frac{3}{4}$

- The power of low sounds
- Strong and weak beats: drums
    - Snare
    - Kick
- Strong and weak beats: $\frac{4}{4}$
    - How to identify time signatures by ear

Workbook

Rhythm 3: How to Understand, Write, and Perform Rests

Rest Tracing Exercises

Trace the following whole rests. Remember, whole rests always hang underneath the 4th line of the staff. There is no answer key for this exercise.

Trace the following half rests. Remember, half rests sit on top of the 3rd line of the staff. No answer key.

Trace the following quarter rests. Refer to page 35 of *The Best Music Theory Book for Beginners 1* for a detailed review of how to write quarter rests. There is no answer key for this exercise.

Tip: Start tracing from the top and work your way down. Make sure to trace the lines so that the rests are not bigger than they need to be.

Continue tracing quarter rests.

Trace and Label the Rests

Trace the following exercise which includes a mix of whole rests, half rests, and quarter rests. After you finish tracing all the rests, write underneath each rest to label their names with the correct letter.

(W = whole rest) (H= half rest) (Q= quarter rest)

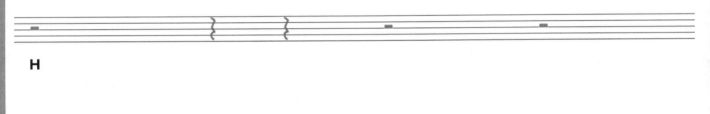

H

Mini quiz 2:

1. Which line do half notes rests sit on top of? _____

2. Which line do whole rests hang below? _____

Spacing Notes and Rests on the Staff

For these next exercises, review p. 39 of The Best Music Theory Book for Beginners for the rules of writing notes and rests, and which beats each type of note and rest can land on. Remember, whole rests show a measure of silence in all time signatures. There are no answer keys for the following exercises.

You must include at least one rest in every measure. There are more than 1 correct answers for many of these exercises. Check your measure math carefully and/or have a coach/teacher review your work. There are no answer keys for these exercises.

Exercise 1

Answer

Remember there are many correct answers. For example measure 1 and measure 5 both have the same numbers written below them, but they have two correct answers that are completely different. There are no answer keys for the following exercises.

Exercise 2

Exercise 3

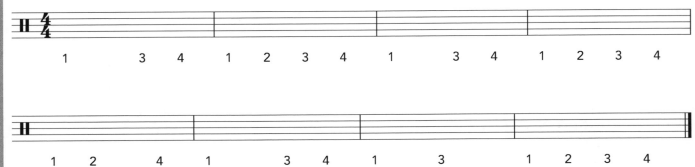

```
1       3   4   1   2   3   4   1       3   4   1   2   3   4
```

```
1   2       4   1       3   4   1       3       1   2   3   4
```

Exercise 4

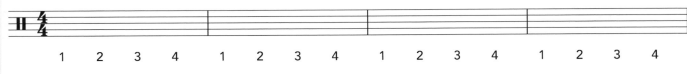

```
1   2   3   4   1   2   3   4   1   2   3   4   1   2   3   4
```

```
1   2   3   4   1   2   3   4   1       3       1   2   3   4
```

Exercise 5

```
1       3   4   1       3       1   2   3   4   1   2   3   4
```

```
1               1   2   3   4   1       3       1   2   3   4
```

Exercise 6

```
1       3       1                   1   2   3   4   1   2   3   4
```

```
1       3       1   2   3   4   1       3       1
```

Exercise 7

1   3   1   2   1   2   3   1   3

1   2   1   2   3   1   3   1   2

Exercise 8

1   3   1   2   1   2   1   3

1   2   1   2   1   3   1   2

Exercise 9

Remember a whole rest can take up an entire measure in any time signature!

1   2   3   1   2   3   1   1   2   3

1   1   2   3   1   2   3   1   2   3

Exercise 10

1   2   3   4   1   3   4   1   1   2   4

1   2   4   1   3   1   3   4   1   3   4

How to Write Lines of Music 2

Exercise 1

In the following two groups of staves in $\frac{4}{4}$, there should be a total of 8 measures in each two-line group. See p. 38 of *The Best Music Theory Book for Beginners 1* for a complete walkthrough. When you are finished, write two of your own rhythmic compositions using whole, half, and quarter notes and rests. Write noteheads on line 3 of the staff with all stems down.

Exercise 2

In the following two groups of $\frac{3}{4}$ staves, there should be a total of 8 measures in each two line group. See p. 38 of *The Best Music Theory Book for Beginners 1* for a complete walkthrough. When you are finished, write two of your own rhythmic compositions using whole, half and quarter rests and half and quarter notes. Write noteheads on line 3 of the staff with all stems down.

Review: Rhythm 3

- Rests
  - Whole rests
  - Half rests
  - Quarter rests

- A whole rest can be used in any time signature to show a full measure of rest

- Measure math 2

- How to write lines of music 2

- How to write notes and rests in a measure

- Where to write notes and rests

- Divide the measure in half in $\frac{4}{4}$

- Composition ideas

New Words You Should Know

1. Rests
2. Composition ideas

Workbook

Rhythm 4: Dots, Ties, Repeat Signs

Writing Dotted Notes

Exercise 1

Trace the dotted half notes.

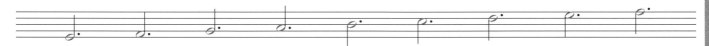

Exercise 2

Trace the dotted half notes then copy them in the same order on the same lines and spaces in the blank spaces to the right of each group of notes.

Exercise 3

Add the dots to the half notes to make dotted half notes. Review the rules for dot writing on p. 44 of *The Best Music Theory Book for Beginners 1*.

Spacing Notes, Dotted Notes, and Rests on the Staff

Now you can use dotted half notes! Remember that a dotted half note will take up an entire measure of $\frac{3}{4}$.

Exercise 1

Use notes only!!!

Exercise 2

Use notes and rests! There is no answer key for this exercise.

Exercise 3

Use notes and rests! There is no answer key for this exercise.

Writing Ties

Remember: You cannot make a tie from a rest to a note or from a note to a rest. You can only tie from one note to another that both on the same line or space of the staff.

Exercise 1

Trace the ties that connect the notes.

Exercise 2

Trace the notes and ties, then copy the tied notes in the blank space to the right of each group of two tied notes. Copy each group of two notes ties together on the same line and space of the staff.

Exercise 3

Add the ties from the last note of the measure to the first note of the next measure for **all measures** that you can add a tie to. Remember you can tie from one line to the next line. You cannot tie from a rest to a note or from a note to a rest.

Writing Repeat Signs

Exercise 1

Trace the repeat signs.

Exercise 2

Trace the repeat signs then copy the repeat signs in the blank space to the right.

Exercise 3

Write a single "end" repeat sign at the end of m. 4. Include a final bar line if needed.

Exercise 4

Write a single "end" repeat sign at the end of m. 2. Include a final bar line if needed.

Exercise 5

Write a "start" repeat sign at the start of m. 2 and an "end" repeat sign at the end of m. 3. Include a final bar line if needed.

Exercise 6

Write a "start" repeat sign at the start of m. 3 and "end" repeat sign at the end of m. 4. Include a final bar line if needed.

Review: Rhythm 4

- Dotted notes

  Dotted half note
  How to write dotted notes
  How to write dotted notes in measures

- Tied Notes

  How to write tied notes
  Tie math
  How to write tied notes in measures
  How to write tied notes in connecting measures
  How to write tied notes from one line of staff to the next
  How to tie more than two notes together

- Repeat signs

  Single repeat sign 1
  Single repeat sign 2
  Double repeat sign 1
  Double repeat sign 2
  How to write repeat signs
  How to write repeat signs at the end of a line of staff
  How to write repeat sings in the middle of a line of staff

- How to write repeat signs over multiple lines of staff

Workbook
Pitch and Notes 1: The Basics

The Basic Musical Alphabet

Write out the basic musical alphabet, filling in the gaps between the letters.

Example

A B C D E F G A B C D E F G A B C D

Ascending (Low to High)

In exercises 1-3 fill in the blanks with the basic musical alphabet from low to high. Count the basic musical alphabet forwards.

Exercise 1

A _____ G _____ B _____ C

Exercise 2

B _____ D _____ C _____ G _____ D

Exercise 3

G _____ F _____ C _____ E

Descending (High to Low)

In exercises 4-6 fill in the blanks with the basic musical alphabet from high to low. Count the basic musical alphabet backwards.

Exercise 4

A _____ F _____ D _____ B _____ G _____ E _____ C _____ A _____ F

Exercise 5

F _____ B _____ E _____ A _____ D

Exercise 6

C _____ D _____ E _____ A

How to Write a Treble Clef

In music, there are several types of clefs. Each one has a unique way to be written. In the following exercises, we will start by practicing writing the Treble (G) Clef.

Review: As with many music theory graphics, there are many ways to write a treble clef. In this exercise, you will practice using this simple five-step process to write great looking treble clefs.

How to Write a Treble Clef

1 Write a curved line from the G line to the B line back to the G line.

2 Write a curved line from the G line to the E line, to the B line.

3 Draw a tilted backward letter S from the B line to above the staff.

4 Draw a line down through the clef to below the staff with a curled end.

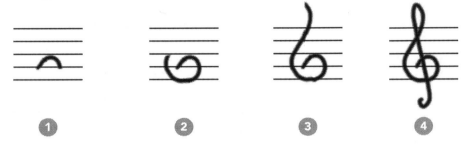

Exercise

Using the above five steps, fill in the following lines of staff with treble clefs. Make sure to follow the steps in order, one by one. There is no answer key for this exercise. Try to make your treble clefs as neat and clear as possible.

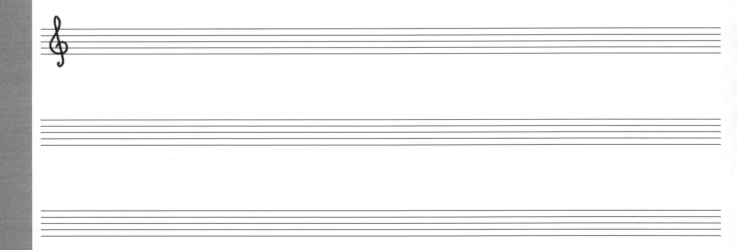

For more information on treble clefs, refer to p. 60 of *The Best Music Theory Book for Beginners 1.*

Note Identification and Writing 1: On the Staff

In the following set of exercises, you will practice identifying notes in the staff and writing them.

Exercise 1

In the first exercises, you will see the notes given on the staff. Write the letter name of the note under the measure in each of the blanks.

Answer

Exercise 2

Write the letter name of the note under the measure in each of the blanks.

Mini quiz 3:

    1. What note name is the first (bottom) line of the staff? _____

    2. What note name is the fourth (second from the top) line of the staff? _____

Exercise 3

Write a quarter note on the staff which matches the letter name under each measure. Remember the correct direction for the stems!

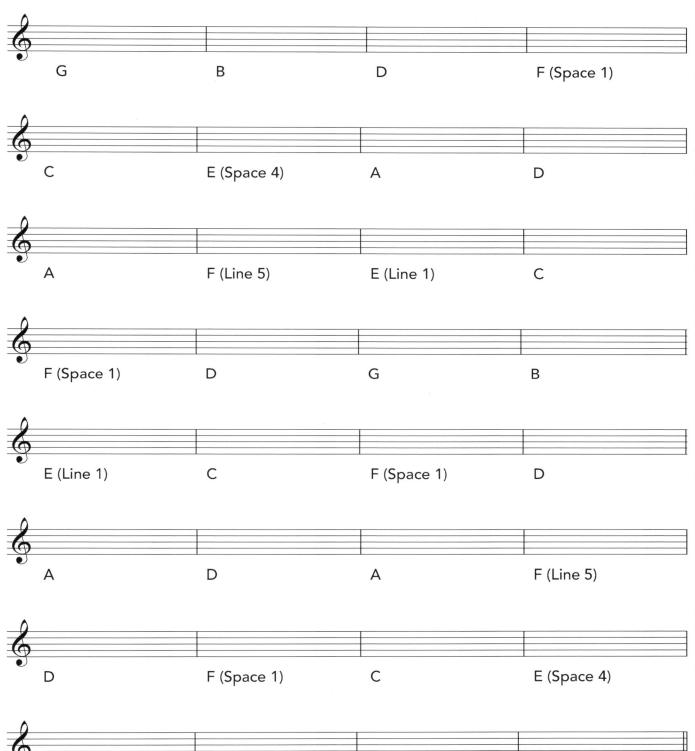

G   B   D   F (Space 1)

C   E (Space 4)   A   D

A   F (Line 5)   E (Line 1)   C

F (Space 1)   D   G   B

E (Line 1)   C   F (Space 1)   D

A   D   A   F (Line 5)

D   F (Space 1)   C   E (Space 4)

D   A   E (Line 1)   C

Note Identification and Writing 2: Ledger Lines

In the following set of exercises, you will practice identifying notes outside of the staff and writing them. Be careful when writing your own ledger lines to make sure that they are straight and the correct length.

For more review on ledger lines, refer to p. 63 of *The Best Music Theory Book for Beginners 1*.

Ascending Ledger Lines   **Descending Ledger Lines**

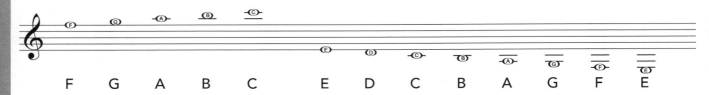

F   G   A   B   C   E   D   C   B   A   G   F   E

Exercise 1

In these exercises, you will see the notes given on ledger lines or just above/below the staff. Write the letter name of the note under the measure in each of the blanks.

Answer

G   C   A   B

B   D   C   A

Exercise 2: Above the Staff

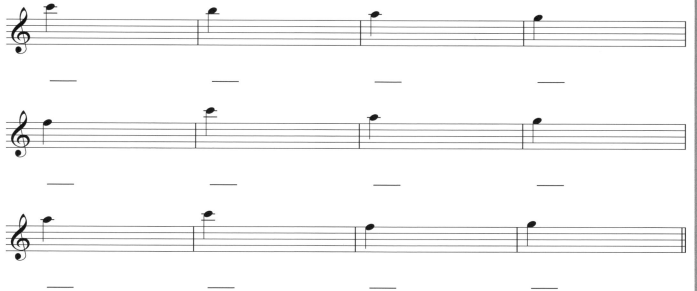

Exercise 2: Below the Staff

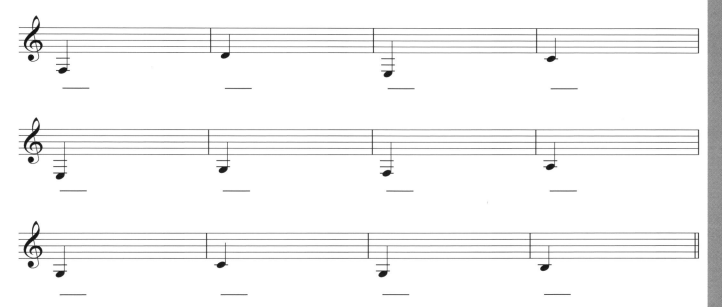

Mini quiz 4:

1. What note name is the space directly below the staff? _____

2. What note name is the space directly above the staff? _____

Exercise 3: Above the Staff

Write a quarter note above the staff which matches the letter name under each measure. Remember the correct direction for the stems!

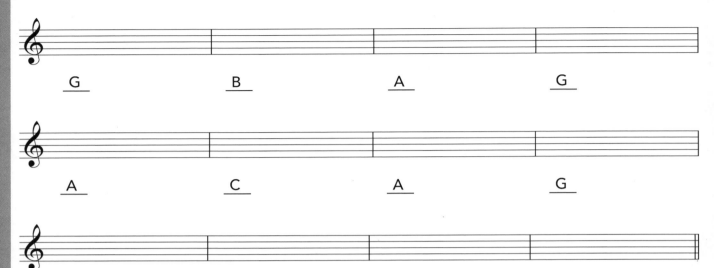

Exercise 3: Below the Staff

Write a quarter note below the staff which matches the letter name under each measure. Remember the correct direction for the stems!

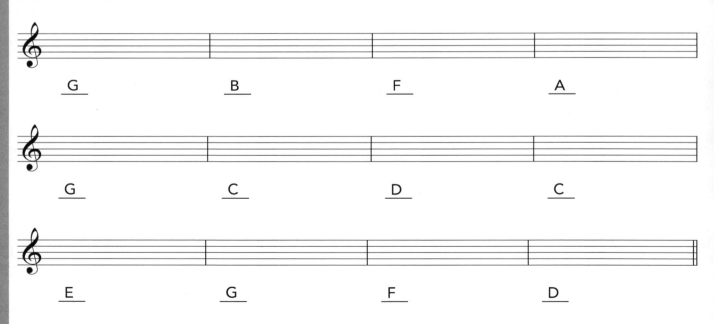

Note Identification and Writing 3: Correct the Errors

In the following worksheets, there are several notes which are labeled incorrectly. This means some of the letter names do not match the notes which are written on the staff.

Example

In these exercises, you will first identify the notes which do not match the letter names written below them by circling the measure. Then, write the letter name which does match the note in the staff.

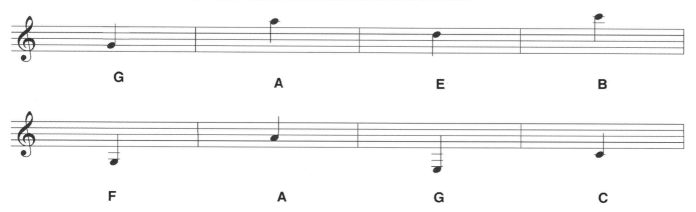

Answer

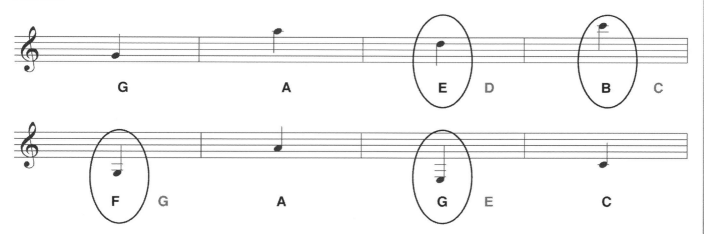

Mini quiz 5:

1. What is the name of the note that is on the third ledger line below the staff? _____

2. What is the name of the note that is on the second ledger line above the staff? _____

Exercise 1

Identify the notes which do not match the letter names written below them by circling the measure. Then, write the letter name which does match the note in the staff.

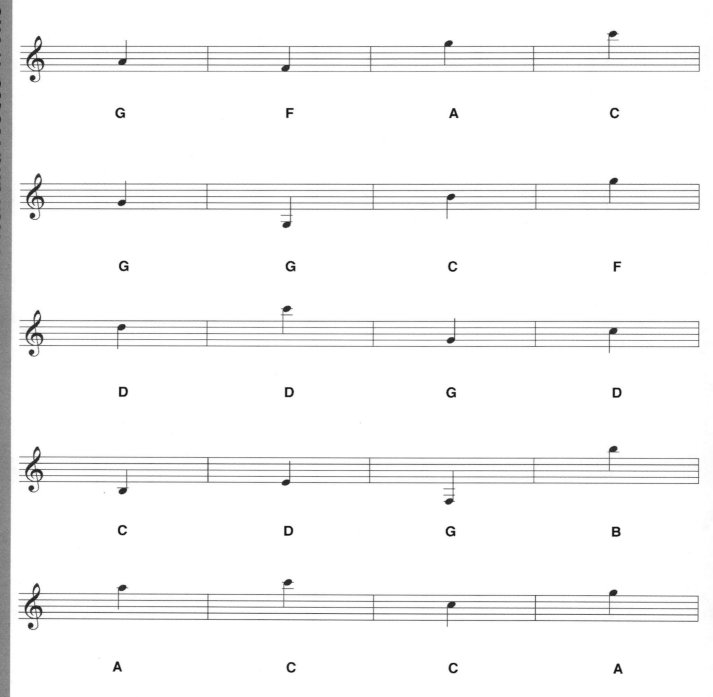

Exercise 2

Identify the notes which do not match the letter names written below them by circling the measure. Then, write the note in the staff (next to the given one) which matches the letter name given.

Review: Pitch and Notes 1

- High vs. low sounds
- How sound is made & measured
    Sound waves

    Hertz

    How sound is made on
    common instruments
- How sound is defined
    Tone

    Timbre
- Melody
- Notes
- The basic musical alphabet
- Notes on the staff
- Treble clef
- How to read notes on the staff
- How to remember notes on the staff
- How to write a treble clef
- Ledger lines

New Words You Should Know

1. Pitch
2. Tone
3. Timbre
4. Melody
5. Notes
6. Treble clef
7. Ledger line

Workbook
Pitch and Notes 2: Theory

Pitch Class

Exercise 1

In every measure there are two notes that are the same pitch class and a third note that is not in the pitch class. Circle the note that does not belong in the pitch class.

Exercise 2

Write all the notes in the pitch class from lowest to highest sounding that we have learned so far. Use quarter notes.

Pitch Class: A
Notes: 3

Pitch Class: C
Notes: 3

Pitch Class: E
Notes: 3

Pitch Class: G
Notes: 3

Pitch Class: B
Notes: 3

Pitch Class: D
Notes: 2

Pitch Class: F
Notes: 3

Pitch Class: A
Notes: 3

Pitch Class: G
Notes: 3

Pitch Class: F
Notes: 3

Pitch Class: E
Notes: 3

Pitch Class: D
Notes: 2

Octave Register

Exercise 1

Label the octave registers for C notes.

C4   C5   C6   __   __   __   __   __   __

Exercise 2

Label the pitch class and octave register for all notes. The register number changes on C.

E3 __ __ __ __ C4 __ __ __ __ C5 __ __ __ __ C6

Exercise 3

Label the pitch class and octave register for all notes. The register number changes on C.

Octaves

Exercise 1

Identify the measures that have octaves by writing a check mark in the "octave" box. If you think the measure does not have an octave in it, check the "not octave" box.

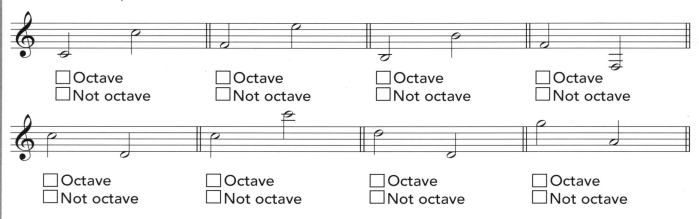

☐ Octave
☐ Not octave

☐ Octave
☐ Not octave

☐ Octave
☐ Not octave

☐ Octave
☐ Not octave

☐ Octave
☐ Not octave

☐ Octave
☐ Not octave

☐ Octave
☐ Not octave

☐ Octave
☐ Not octave

Exercise 2

Write a half note one octave higher and to the right of the note provided. The first measure is an example.

Exercise 3

Write a half note one octave lower and to the right of the note provided. The first measure is an example.

Accidentals

Exercise 1

Trace the accidentals.

Exercise 2

Trace then the accidentals and notes, then copy the notes and accidentals in the blank space to the right of each group of notes. Copy the notes onto the same lines and spaces of the staff.

Exercise 3

Write a half note with an accidental in the indicated octave register.

F♯4   C♯5   B♭4   F♯5   F♯4   C♯6   F♯3   F♯5

F♯3   F♯4   B♭3   F♯5   F♯3   C♯4   F♯4   F♯5

Courtesy Accidentals

Exercise 1

Identify the correct and wrong accidentals and courtesy accidentals by putting a check in the check box under each note that has a check box. Review p. 71, 72 of *The Best Music Theory Book for Beginners 1*.

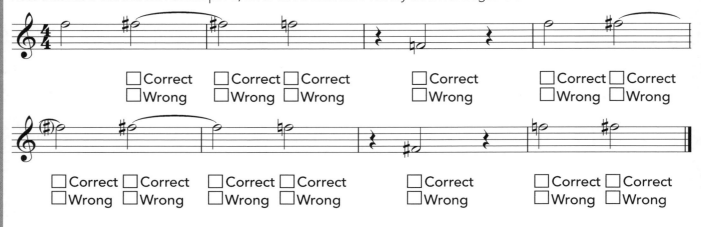

☐ Correct   ☐ Correct ☐ Correct   ☐ Correct   ☐ Correct ☐ Correct
☐ Wrong   ☐ Wrong ☐ Wrong   ☐ Wrong   ☐ Wrong ☐ Wrong

☐ Correct ☐ Correct   ☐ Correct ☐ Correct   ☐ Correct   ☐ Correct ☐ Correct
☐ Wrong ☐ Wrong   ☐ Wrong ☐ Wrong   ☐ Wrong   ☐ Wrong ☐ Wrong

Exercise 2

Write in the "natural" courtesy accidentals where they should go.

Exercise 3

Write in the "natural" courtesy accidentals where they should go.

The Full Musical Alphabet

Write out the basic musical alphabet, filling in the gaps between the letters.

Example

A A#/Bb B C C#/Db D D#/Eb E F F#/Gb G#/A A A#/Bb B C C#/Db D D#/Eb E F F#/Gb G#/A A A#/Bb

Ascending (Low to High)

In exercises 1-3 fill in the blanks with the full musical alphabet from low to high. Count the full musical alphabet forwards.

Exercise 1

A		C		D#/Eb		F#/Gb			A#/Bb	C#/Db		E		G		A#/Bb

Exercise 2

A		C#/Db		F			A#/Bb		D		F#/Gb		A#/Bb

Exercise 3

A		D		G		C		F		A#/Bb

Descending (High to Low)

In exercises 4-6 fill in the blanks with the full musical alphabet from high to low. Count the full musical alphabet backwards.

Exercise 4

A	G	F	D#/Eb	C#/Db	B	A	G	F	D	C	A#/Bb	G#/Ab

Exercise 5

A		F#/Gb		D#/Eb		C		G#/Ab		F		D		B		G#/Ab

Exercise 6

A		F		C#/Db		G#/Ab		E		C		G#/Ab

Writing Half Steps

Exercise 1

Identify the half steps. Mark the check box "Half Step" if the two notes in the measure are one half step apart. Mark the box "Not" if the two notes in a measure are not one half step apart.

☐ Half Step ☐ Half Step ☐ Half Step ☐ Half Step ☐ Half Step ☐ Half Step ☐ Half Step ☐ Half Step
☐ Not ☐ Not ☐ Not ☐ Not ☐ Not ☐ Not ☐ Not ☐ Not

☐ Half Step ☐ Half Step ☐ Half Step ☐ Half Step ☐ Half Step ☐ Half Step ☐ Half Step ☐ Half Step
☐ Not ☐ Not ☐ Not ☐ Not ☐ Not ☐ Not ☐ Not ☐ Not

Exercise 2

Write a note one half step higher than the provided note in the same measure. Use the enharmonic equivalent note name that has the next letter in the musical alphabet (A to B♭, not A to A♯). Use only the **common** enharmonic equivalents. The first measure is an example.

Exercise 3

Write a note one half step lower than the provided note. Use the enharmonic equivalent note name that has the next letter in the musical alphabet (A to G♯, not A to A♭). Use only the **common** enharmonic equivalents. The first measure is an example.

Writing Whole Steps

Exercise 1

Identify the whole steps.

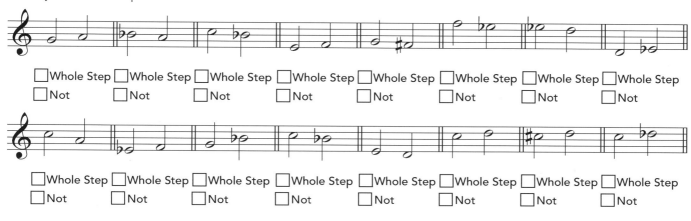

☐ Whole Step ☐ Whole Step ☐ Whole Step ☐ Whole Step ☐ Whole Step ☐ Whole Step ☐ Whole Step ☐ Whole Step
☐ Not ☐ Not ☐ Not ☐ Not ☐ Not ☐ Not ☐ Not ☐ Not

☐ Whole Step ☐ Whole Step ☐ Whole Step ☐ Whole Step ☐ Whole Step ☐ Whole Step ☐ Whole Step ☐ Whole Step
☐ Not ☐ Not ☐ Not ☐ Not ☐ Not ☐ Not ☐ Not ☐ Not

Exercise 2

Write a note one whole step higher than the provided note in the same measure. Use the enharmonic equivalent note name that has the next letter in the musical alphabet (F♯ to G♯, not F♯ to A♭). Use only the **common** enharmonic equivalents. The first measure is an example.

Exercise 3

Write a note one whole step lower than the provided note. Use the enharmonic equivalent note name that has the next letter in the musical alphabet. Use only the **common** enharmonic equivalents (G♯ to F♯, not G♯ to G♭). The first measure is an example.

Pitch Class 2

Exercise 1

In every measure there are two notes that are the same pitch class and a third note that is not in the pitch class. Circle the note that does not belong in the pitch class.

Exercise 2

Write all the notes in the pitch class from lowest to highest sounding that we have learned so far. Use quarter notes.

| Pitch Class: A | Pitch Class: C | Pitch Class: E | Pitch Class: G |
| Notes: 3 | Notes: 3 | Notes: 3 | Notes: 3 |

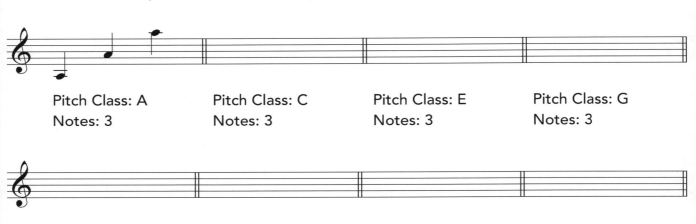

| Pitch Class: F♯ | Pitch Class: D | Pitch Class: F | Pitch Class: B |
| Notes: 3 | Notes: 2 | Notes: 3 | Notes: 3 |

| Pitch Class: G | Pitch Class: F | Pitch Class: F♯ | Pitch Class: D |
| Notes: 3 | Notes: 3 | Notes: 3 | Notes: 2 |

Review: Pitch and Notes 2

- The 12-key pattern
- The basic musical alphabet on the keyboard
- Pitch class
- Octave register
- Octaves
- Accidentals
- How to write accidentals
  How to write accidentals in front of notes
  How to write accidentals in a measure
- Courtesy accidentals
  How to write courtesy accidentals in a measure
- Enharmonic equivalents
- The full musical alphabet: the 12 notes of music
- Half step
- Whole step

New Words You Should Know

1. Pitch class
2. Octave register
3. Octave
4. Accidentals
5. Flat
6. Natural
7. Sharp
8. Courtesy accidentals
9. Enharmonic
10. Half step
11. Whole step

Workbook
Pitch and Notes 3: Scales

Writing Chromatic Scales

Exercise 1

Write an ascending chromatic scale with sharp and natural accidentals. The first and last notes are already there.

Exercise 2

Write an ascending chromatic scale with sharp and natural accidentals. The first and last notes are already there.

Exercise 3

Write an ascending chromatic scale with flat and natural accidentals. The first and last notes are already there.

Exercise 4

Write an ascending chromatic scale with flat and natural accidentals. The first and last notes are already there.

Exercise 5

Write a descending chromatic scale with sharp and natural accidentals. The first and last notes are already there.

Exercise 6

Write a descending chromatic scale with flat and natural accidentals. The first and last notes are already there.

Major Scale, Write Scale Degrees

C Major Scale Degrees

Write the scale degrees in the blanks under the staff. C is always $\hat{1}$. It does not matter which octave the note is written in. Think of the pitch class and write the scale degree that the pitch class of the note belongs to.

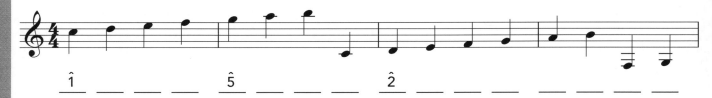

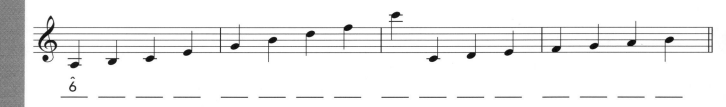

G Major Scale Degrees

Write the scale degrees in the blanks under the staff. G is always $\hat{1}$. It does not matter which octave the note is written in. Think of the pitch class and write the scale degree that the pitch class of the note belongs to.

Write Major Scales with Accidentals

Review p. 82 in *The Best Music Theory Book for Beginners 1* for a step by step example and walk-through.

Exercise 1

In exercises 1, 2, 3, and 4, write a major scale starting on the note provided and add accidentals. Use whole notes. For extra credit, write the scale degrees below each note of the scale.

Exercise 2

Exercise 3

Exercise 4

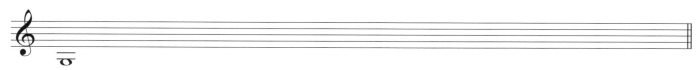

Exercise 5

In exercises 5, 6, and 7, write either a C or G major scale with accidentals. For extra credit, write the scale degrees below each note of the scale. Remember to write a treble clef and double barline. There is no answer key for 5-7.

Exercise 6

Exercise 7

Names of Major Scale Degrees

Exercise 1

Write in the scale degree names for each note as if the note was a part of the C major scale. All scale degree names can be found on p. 84 of *The Best Music Theory Book for Beginners 1*.

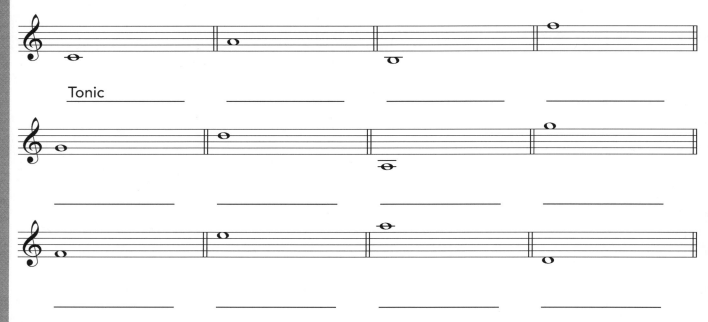

Tonic _____ _____ _____

Exercise 2

Write in the scale degree names for each note as if they are in a G major scale.

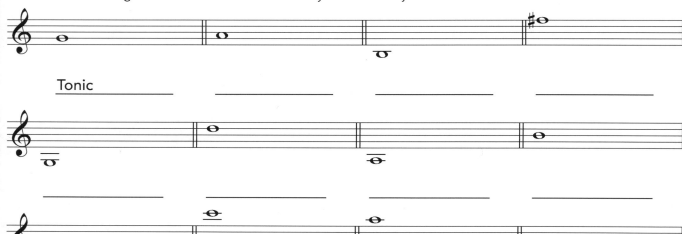

Tonic _____ _____ _____

Writing Tetrachords

Exercise 1

Write a G major tetrachord with quarter notes.

Exercise 2

Write a C major tetrachord with quarter notes.

Exercise 3

Write a G major tetrachord after the C major tetrachord to complete the C major scale with quarter notes.

Exercise 4

Write a C major tetrachord before the G major tetrachord to complete the C major scale with quarter notes.

Exercise 5

Write a G major tetrachord before the D major tetrachord to complete the G major scale with quarter notes.

Writing Major Key Signatures

In this book, we will focus only on the major keys of C and G. In later books, additional keys will be introduced, as well as easy step by step processes to identify them.

Let's start by reviewing what you learned on p.86 of *The Best Music Theory Book for Beginners 1* about key signatures.

Exercise 1

Which key signature is written in the measure below (no sharps or flats)?

Key of _____

Exercise 2

Which key signature is written in the measure below (1 sharp)?

Key of _____

Exercise 3

Which note needs a sharp in the example below in order to make this match the key of G? Add the sharp on the staff next to the note which needs it.

___#

Exercise 4

The key below should be C. Which notes in the scale below are **not** in the key of C?

___#, ___#, and ___#

Exercise 5

In the next 8 measures, write the key signature in each measure for the key of G, and label underneath the measure which key it is. The first measure is already completed for you. There is a reminder in the 5th measure to help you.

Key of G

Exercise 6

In the next 8 measures, write the key signature in each measure for the key of C, and label underneath the measure which key it is. The first measure is already completed for you.

Key of C

Writing Major Scales with Key Signatures

Review p. 88-89 in *The Best Music Theory Book for Beginners 1* for a step by step example and walk-through.

Exercise 1

In exercises 1, 2, 3, and 4, write a key signature and major scale starting on the note provided. Use whole notes.

Exercise 2

Exercise 3

Exercise 4

Exercise 5

In exercises 5, 6, and 7, write either a C or G major scale with a key signature. Make sure to write a treble clef at the left end of the staff and a double bar line at the right side end of the staff. There is no answer key for Exercises 5-7.

Exercise 6

Exercise 7

Natural Minor Scale, Write Scale Degrees

A Natural Minor Scale Degrees

Write the scale degrees in the blanks under the staff. A is always $\hat{1}$. It does not matter which octave the note is written in. Think of the pitch class and write the scale degree that the pitch class of the note belongs to.

E Natural Minor Scale Degrees

Write the scale degrees in the blanks under the staff. E is always $\hat{1}$. It does not matter which octave the note is written in. Think of the pitch class and write the scale degree that the pitch class of the note belongs to.

Relative Keys and Scales

For more information on relative keys and scales, refer to p. 92-94 of *The Best Music Theory Book for Beginners 1*.

Example: With Accidentals

Step 1-3

Step 4

Exercise 1

Step 1

Write the first note of the C major scale below the staff (C4). Write the next six notes of the **basic** musical alphabet.

Step 2

Write the C major scale (C4-C5) up to $\hat{1}$ ($\hat{8}$). Write in any accidentals needed. (Are there accidentals in C major?)

Step 3

Now, we're going to write the relative minor of C, which is A natural minor. First, copy the C major scale you wrote in Step 2, and now circle the 6th note of the scale which is $\hat{6}$.

Step 4

Finally, write the musical alphabet starting on the note which you circled in step 3. Then, add the same accidentals which you wrote in Step 2. (Are there any sharps or flats in this scale?). This is the A natural minor scale.

Exercise 2

Step 1

Start by writing the first note of the G major scale below the second ledger line below the staff (G3). Then, write the next six notes of the **basic** musical alphabet, going up one by one. Don't worry about accidentals. We will add them in the next step.

Step 2

Write the G major scale (G3-G4) up to $\hat{1}(\hat{8})$. Then, write in any accidentals needed for the scale. You can think about which accidentals are needed to write the key signature for the G major scale, then add those in if any.

Step 3

Now, we're going to write the relative minor of G, which is E natural minor. First, copy the G major scale you wrote in Step 2 up to $\hat{6}$, including any accidentals, and circle the 6th note of the scale, which is $\hat{6}$.

Step 4

Finally, write the musical alphabet starting on the note which you circled in step 3. Then, add the same accidentals which you added in Step 2 to the same pitch class(es). This is the E natural minor scale.

Example: With Key Signatures

Step 1-2

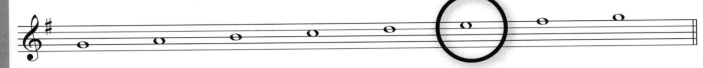

Step 3

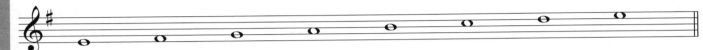

Exercise 3

Step 1

Start by writing the key signature for C major and the first note of the C major scale below the staff (C4). Then, write the next six notes of the **basic** musical alphabet, going up one by one. Don't worry about accidentals, they are shown in the key signature.

Step 2

Now, we're going to write the relative minor of C, which is A natural minor. First, copy the key signature and C major scale you wrote in Step 1 (C4-C5) up to $\hat{1}(\hat{8})$. Now circle the 6th note of the scale, $\hat{6}$.

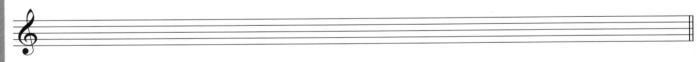

Step 3

Finally, write the same key signature as Steps 1-2, write the **basic** musical alphabet starting on the note which you circled in Step 2 ($\hat{6}$) up to the same pitch class one octave higher.

Exercise 4

Step 1

Start by writing the key signature for G major and the first note of the G major scale below the second ledger line below the staff (G3). Then, write the next six notes of the **basic** musical alphabet, going up one by one. Don't worry about accidentals, they are shown in the key signature.

Step 2

Now, we're going to write the relative minor of G, which is E natural minor. First, copy the key signature and G major scale you wrote in Step 1 (G3-G4) up to $\hat{1}$ ($\hat{8}$) . Now circle the 6th note of the scale, $\hat{6}$.

Step 3

Finally, write the same key signature as Steps 1-2, and write the **basic** musical alphabet starting on the note which you circled in Step 2 ($\hat{6}$) up to the same pitch class one octave higher.

Write the Note Names C Major and A Natural Minor

Fill in the blanks with the correct note names to complete the major scale or the relative natural minor scale.

Scale Degree	$\hat{1}$	$\hat{2}$	$\hat{3}$	$\hat{4}$	$\hat{5}$	$\hat{6}$	$\hat{7}$
Note Name		D		F			B

	$\hat{6}$	$\hat{7}$					
Scale Degree	A		$\hat{1}$	$\hat{2}$	$\hat{3}$	$\hat{4}$	$\hat{5}$
Note Name			C		E		G

Scale Degree	$\hat{6}$	$\hat{7}$	$\hat{1}$	$\hat{2}$	$\hat{3}$	$\hat{4}$	$\hat{5}$
Note Name	A				E		

Scale Degree	$\hat{1}$	$\hat{2}$	$\flat\hat{3}$	$\hat{4}$	$\hat{5}$	$\flat\hat{6}$	$\flat\hat{7}$
Note Name	A	B				F	G

Relative Key Signatures

1. Write a treble clef.

2. Write the key signature.

C Major

A Minor

G Major

E Minor

A Minor

E Minor

C Major

G Major

Relative Step Formula

Write in either "Whole" or "Half" in the blank boxes where the whole or half step should go to complete the major step formula or the natural minor step formula.

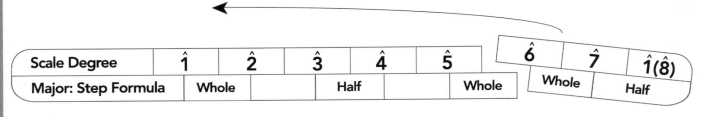

Scale Degree	$\hat{1}$	$\hat{2}$	$\hat{3}$	$\hat{4}$	$\hat{5}$	$\hat{6}$	$\hat{7}$	$\hat{1}(\hat{8})$
Major: Step Formula	Whole		Half		Whole	Whole	Half	

Scale Degree	$\hat{6}$	$\hat{7}$	$\hat{1}$	$\hat{2}$	$\hat{3}$	$\hat{4}$	$\hat{5}$	$\hat{6}$
Major: Step Formula	Whole	Half			Half		Whole	

Scale Degree	$\hat{6}$	$\hat{7}$	$\hat{1}$	$\hat{2}$	$\hat{3}$	$\hat{4}$	$\hat{5}$	$\hat{6}$
Major: Step Formula	Whole	Half						I

Scale Degree	$\hat{1}$	$\hat{2}$	$\flat\hat{3}$	$\hat{4}$	$\hat{5}$	$\flat\hat{6}$	$\flat\hat{7}$	$\hat{1}(\hat{8})$
Minor: Step Formula			Whole				Whole	

Writing Natural Minor Scales with Accidentals

Review p. 95-96 in *The Best Music Theory Book for Beginners 1* for a step by step example and walk-through.

Exercise 1

In exercises 1, 2, 3, and 4, write a natural minor scale starting on the note provided and add accidentals. Use whole notes. For extra credit, write the scale degree numbers below each note of the scale.

Exercise 2

Exercise 3

Exercise 4

Exercise 5

In exercises 5, 6, and 7, write either an A or E natural minor scale with accidentals. For extra credit, write the scale degrees below each note of the scale. Make sure to write a treble clef at the left end of the staff. There are no answer keys for exercises 5-7.

Exercise 6

Exercise 7

Writing Natural Minor Scales with Key Signatures

Review p. 97 in *The Best Music Theory Book for Beginners 1* for a step by step example and walk-through.

Exercise 1

In exercises 1, 2, 3, and 4, write a key signature and natural minor scale starting on the note provided.
Use whole notes.

Exercise 2

Exercise 3

Exercise 4

Exercise 5

In exercises 5, 6, and 7, write either an A or E natural minor scale with a key signature. Make sure to write a treble clef at the left end of the staff. There are no answer keys for exercises 5-7.

Exercise 6

Exercise 7

Names of Natural Minor Scale Degrees

Exercise 1

Write in the scale degree names for each note as if they were a part of an A natural minor scale. Scale degree names for each note can be found on p. 98 of *The Best Music Theory Book for Beginners 1*.

Tonic _____   _____   _____   _____

_____   _____   _____   _____

_____   _____   _____   _____

Exercise 2

Write in the scale degree names for each note as if they were a part of an E natural minor scale.

Tonic _____   _____   _____   _____

_____   _____   _____   _____

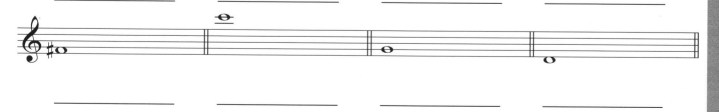

_____   _____   _____   _____

Writing Pentachords

Exercise 1

In exercises 1, 2, 3, and 4, write a minor pentachord starting from the note provided using whole notes and accidentals if needed. Label the whole and half steps below the notes. Label the scale degree numbers below the staff.

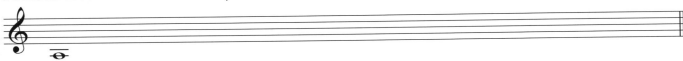

Exercise 2

Exercise 3

Exercise 4

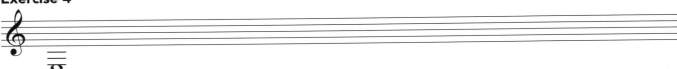

Exercise 5

In exercises 1, 2, 3, and 4, write a major pentachord starting from the note provided using accidentals if needed. Label the whole and half steps along with scale degrees.

Exercise 6

Exercise 7

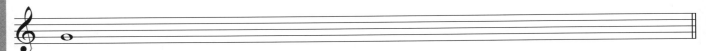

Exercise 8

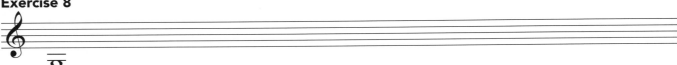

Review: Pitch and Notes 3

- Chromatic scale
- How to write chromatic scales
    - How to write a chromatic scale with flats
    - How to write a chromatic scale with sharps
- Scale degrees
    - Why we use scale degrees
    - How to identify scale degrees
    - What happens to the starting pitch class?
    - How to write scale degrees
- Diatonic major scales 1
- How to write major scales
    - Ascending
    - Descending
- Scale degree names
    - Tonic
    - Supertonic
    - Mediant
    - Subdomiant
    - Dominant
    - Submediant
    - Leading tone
- Tetrachords
- Key signatures 1
    - How to identify key signatures
    - How to write key signatures
- How to write major scales with key signatures
    - Ascending
    - Descending
    - Ascending + descending
- The Natural Minor Scale
- Compare major and minor scales
    - Scale quality
    - Scale degrees
- How to write natural minor scales
    - Ascending
    - Descending
    - Ascending + descending

New Words You Should Know

1. Scale
2. Chromatic
3. Tonic
4. Supertonic
5. Mediant
6. Subdomiant
7. Dominant
8. Submediant
9. Leading tone
10. Subtonic
11. Key signature
12. Scale quality
13. Relative keys
14. Tetrachord
15. Pentachord

Workbook
Pitch and Notes 4: Simple Intervals

Interval Identification 1

Interval Direction

Exercise 1

Label the direction of the interval as asc., dsc., or hrm.

asc. _____   _____ _____ _____   _____

_____ _____   _____ _____   _____   _____

_____ _____   _____ _____   _____

Interval Quality

Exercise 1

Write the abbreviation for the quality in the blank space.

Major_____   minor_____   Perfect_____   diminished_____   Augmented_____

Exercise 2

Write the abbreviations for the possible qualities for each interval. If an interval can be both m and M, write m first, then M.

U can be_____   2 can be_____, _____   3 can be_____, _____   4 can be_____, _____

5 can be_____, _____   6 can be_____, _____   7 can be_____, _____   8 can be_____

Interval Identification 2: Harmonic Intervals

Key: C Major

In this section, you will practice one of the most fundamentally important things to understand; harmonic intervals. In these exercises, you will learn how to identify harmonic intervals step by step. The days of guessing which harmonic interval you're looking at will be long gone after you take the time to understand these steps. You are now entering "easy major scale land" where intervals can only be "M" or "P".

Step 1

Pay attention to the bottom note of the interval. In this example, it is C.

Step 2

Write out the major scale for the note on the bottom. In this case, it will be a C major scale. Circle the bottom note (C, in this case) and the top note of the interval (A, in this case).

Note- once you have learned and memorized all the major scales, you can skip to step 4. This is because once you have memorized them all, you should be able to think of the notes in your head without needing to write out the whole scale.

Step 3

Remember, every interval has a number which tells you the distance between the two letters in the musical alphabet. To figure out this number, start on the bottom note (C) as 1. Then, count up the scale until you arrive to the note which is on top (A) of the interval. (Think: C, 1.... D, 2... E, 3... until you get A, 6.) Now we know that the interval is some kind of 6th (either major or minor).

Step 4

The last step after identifying the number (6th) is to determine the quality of the interval. This step is surprisingly simple. All you need to do is refer to the major scale which you wrote down in step 2. If the note on the top of the interval matches the note in the scale (i.e. it doesn't have any accidental which is different) then it's major or perfect, because all the asc. + hrm. intervals in a major scale are either major or perfect. In this case, since it's a 6th, it's major.

Major 6th (hrm. M6)

Exercise 1

In the following exercises, you will use the steps from before to identify the following intervals in the key of C.

Step 1

Pay attention to the bottom note of the interval. Write the letter name here _____

Step 2

Write the major scale for the bottom note with quarter notes. Circle the bottom + top note of the interval from Step 1.

Step 3

Count from the bottom note of the interval up the scale until you get to the top note.

Write the number of the interval here _____

Step 4

Is the quality of the interval M or P?

Write your answer here _____

Exercise 2

Step 1

Pay attention to the bottom note of the interval. Write the letter name here _____

Step 2

Write the major scale for the bottom note with quarter notes. Circle the bottom + top note of the interval from Step 1.

Step 3

Count from the bottom note of the interval up the scale until you get to the top note.

Write the number (distance) of the interval here _____

Step 4

Is the quality of the interval M or P?

Write your answer here _____

Tip: Remember that when you compare any note from any major scale to its root (for example, comparing any note of the C major scale to the note C) the quality of the interval will always be either major or perfect. Perfect intervals: Unison (U), Fourth (4), Fifth (5), and Octave (8) Major intervals: Second (2), Third (3), Sixth (6), and Seventh (7).

Exercise 3

In the following exercises, you will use the steps from before to identify the following intervals in the keys of C.

Step 1

Pay attention to the bottom note of the interval. Write the letter name here _____

Step 2

Write the major scale for the bottom note with quarter notes. Circle the bottom + top note of the interval from Step 1.

Step 3

Count from the bottom note of the interval up the scale until you get to the top note.

Write the number (distance) of the interval here _____

Step 4

Is the quality of the interval M or P?

Write your answer here _____

Exercise 4

Step 1

Pay attention to the bottom note of the interval. Write the letter name here _____

Step 2

Write the major scale for the bottom note with quarter notes. Circle the bottom + top note of the interval from Step 1.

Step 3

Count from the bottom note of the interval up the scale until you get to the top note.

Write the number (distance) of the interval here _____

Step 4

Is the quality of the interval M or P?

Write your answer here _____

Exercise 5

In the following exercises, you will use the steps from before to identify the following intervals in the keys of C.

Step 1

Pay attention to the bottom note of the interval. Write the letter name here _____

Step 2

Write the major scale for the bottom note with quarter notes. Circle the bottom + top note of the interval from Step 1.

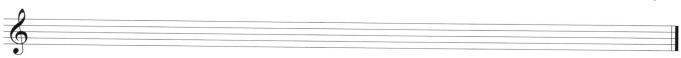

Step 3

Count from the bottom note of the interval up the scale until you get to the top note.

Write the number (distance) of the interval here _____

Step 4

Is the quality of the interval M or P?

Write your answer here _____

Exercise 6

Step 1

Pay attention to the bottom note of the interval. Write the letter name here _____

Step 2

Write the major scale for the bottom note with quarter notes. Circle the bottom + top note of the interval from Step 1.

Step 3

Count from the bottom note of the interval up the scale until you get to the top note.

Write the number (distance) of the interval here _____

Step 4

Is the quality of the interval M or P?

Write your answer here _____

Key: G Major

In the last section, you practiced identifying intervals in the key of C. Now, you will apply the same steps as you did in the key of C, only this time in the key of G. You are in "easy major scale land" where intervals can only be "M" or "P".

In these exercises, you will apply the same step by step process as before in the key of G.

Step 1

Pay attention to the bottom note of the interval. In this example, it is G.

Step 2

Write out the major scale for the note on the bottom. In this case, it will be a G major scale. Circle the bottom note (G, in this case) and the top note of the interval (F#, in this case).

Note- once you have learned and memorized all the major scales, you can skip to step 4. This is because once you have memorized them all, you should be able to think of the notes in your head without needing to write out the whole scale.

Step 3

Remember, every interval has a number which tells you the distance between the two letters in the musical alphabet. To figure out this number, start on the bottom note (G) as 1. Then, count up the scale until you arrive to the note which is on top (F#) of the interval. (Think: G, 1.... A, 2... B, 3... until you get F#, 7.) Now we know that the interval is some kind of 7th (either major or minor).

Step 4

The last step after identifying the number (7th) is to determine the quality of the interval. This step is surprisingly simple. All you need to do is refer to the major scale which you wrote down in step 2. If the note on the top of the interval matches the note in the scale (i.e. it doesn't have any accidental which is different) then it's major or perfect, because all the asc. + hrm. intervals in a major scale are either major or perfect. In this case, since it's a 7th, it's Major.

Major 7th (hrm. M7)

Exercise 1

In the following exercises, you will use the steps from before to identify the following intervals in the key of G.

Step 1

Pay attention to the bottom note of the interval. Write the letter name here _____

Step 2

Write the major scale for the bottom note with quarter notes. Circle the bottom + top note of the interval from Step 1.

Step 3

Count from the bottom note of the interval up the scale until you get to the top note.

Write the number (distance) of the interval here _____

Step 4

Is the quality of the interval M or P?

Write your answer here _____

Exercise 2

Step 1

Pay attention to the bottom note of the interval. Write the letter name here _____

Step 2

Write the major scale for the bottom note with quarter notes. Circle the bottom + top note of the interval from Step 1.

Step 3

Count from the bottom note of the interval up the scale until you get to the top note.

Write the number (distance) of the interval here _____

Step 4

Is the quality of the interval M or P?

Write your answer here _____

Tip: Remember that when you compare any note from any major scale to its root (for example, comparing any note of the C major scale to the note C) the quality of the interval will always be either major or perfect. Perfect intervals: Unison (U), Fourth (4), Fifth (5), and Octave (8) Major intervals: Second (2), Third (3), Sixth (6), and Seventh (7).

Exercise 3

In the following exercises, you will use the steps from before to identify the following intervals in the keys of G.

Step 1

Pay attention to the bottom note of the interval. Write the letter name here _____

Step 2

Write the major scale for the bottom note with quarter notes. Circle the bottom + top note of the interval from Step 1.

Step 3

Count from the bottom note of the interval up the scale until you get to the top note.

Write the number (distance) of the interval here _____

Step 4

Is the quality of the interval M or P?

Write your answer here _____

Exercise 4

Step 1

Pay attention to the bottom note of the interval. Write the letter name here _____

Step 2

Write the major scale for the bottom note with quarter notes. Circle the bottom + top note of the interval from Step 1.

Step 3

Count from the bottom note of the interval up the scale until you get to the top note.

Write the number (distance) of the interval here _____

Step 4

Is the quality of the interval M or P?

Write your answer here _____

Exercise 5

In the following exercises, you will use the steps from before to identify the following intervals in the keys of G.

Step 1

Pay attention to the bottom note of the interval. Write the letter name here _____

Step 2

Write the major scale for the bottom note with quarter notes. Circle the bottom + top note of the interval from Step 1.

Step 3

Count from the bottom note of the interval up the scale until you get to the top note.

Write the number (distance) of the interval here _____

Step 4

Is the quality of the interval M or P?

Write your answer here _____

Exercise 6

Step 1

Pay attention to the bottom note of the interval. Write the letter name here _____

Step 2

Write the major scale for the bottom note with quarter notes. Circle the bottom + top note of the interval from Step 1.

Step 3

Count from the bottom note of the interval up the scale until you get to the top note.

Write the number (distance) of the interval here _____

Step 4

Is the quality of the interval M or P?

Write your answer here _____

Now that you have practiced basic intervals in the earlier section of this book, and have practiced the G major scale and C major scale, now it's time to practice identifying intervals with ledger lines. Remember to follow the steps to identify intervals which you practiced in the earlier section.

Example
Label the following intervals with their quality: M for major and P for perfect. Make sure to also include the distance (2, 3, 4, 5, 6, 7) of the interval as well.

M3   P5   M7   P5

Exercise 1
Label the following intervals with M for major and P for perfect. Make sure to also include the distance of the interval as well. All of these exercises are based on the key of C. Write the labels of the intervals below the staff.

Exercise 2
Label the following intervals with M for major and P for perfect. Make sure to also include the distance of the interval as well. All of these exercises are based on the key of G. Write the labels of the intervals below the staff.

How to Think About Writing and Labeling Harmonic and Ascending Intervals Reminder 1

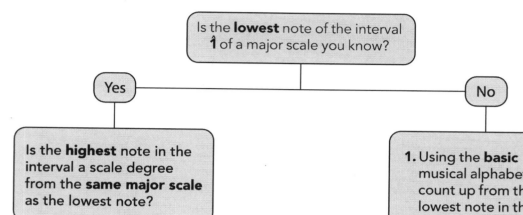

Is the **lowest** note of the interval î of a major scale you know?

Yes

No

Is the **highest** note in the interval a scale degree from the **same major scale** as the lowest note?

Yes

No

Yes branch:

1. The lowest note in the interval is the tonic of the major scale you will use. Think of the lowest note as î.

2. Count **up** the major scale of the lowest note up it's scale until you get to the highest (top) note of the interval counting scale degree numbers. Remember the scale degree number for the highest (top) note of the interval.

3. Write or label the interval with direction (asc., hrm., U) quality (**U, M, P**), and distance (scale degree number of the highest note).

No branch:

1. Using the **basic** musical alphabet count up from the lowest note in the interval to the highest note and figure out the "some kind of" interval. p.105

2. Which qualities could be used for the "some kind of" interval that you figured out? p. 104

3. Count the half steps to know the quality of the interval using the **full** musical alphabet and look at p. 106.

4. Write or label the interval with direction (asc. ,hrm. U) quality (**U, m, M, P, A, d**), and distance.

No (right) branch:

1. Using the **basic** musical alphabet count up from the lowest note in the interval to the highest note and figure out the "some kind of" interval. p.105

2. Which qualities could be used for the "some kind of" interval that you figured out? p. 104

3. Count the half steps to know the quality of the interval using the **full** musical alphabet and look at p. 106.

4. Write or label the interval with direction (asc. ,hrm. U) quality (**U, m, M, P, A, d**), and distance.

More Harmonic Intervals

You are no longer in "easy major scale land" and qualities can be m, M, P, A, and d. Uses p. 104-106 of *The Best Music Theory Book for Beginners 1*.

1. Figure out interval direction. p. 104.

2. Figure out the "some kind of" (use the **basic** musical alphabet, the lowest note is 1). p.105.

3. Which qualities could be used for the "some kind of" interval distance? p.106.

4. Figure out whole or half steps to know the quality of the interval (use the **full** musical alphabet). Compare with p.106.

5. Write the interval with direction, quality, and distance.

hrm. P5

Interval Identification 3: Ascending Intervals

Key: C Major

Exercise

In the following exercises, you will use the steps from before to identify the following intervals in the key of C major. Remember you can count up the major scale just like you did for the harmonic intervals. Now, follow the same steps as for figuring out the harmonic intervals in your head. Label melodic unisons as just "PU". You are now in "easy major scale land" and qualities will only be "M" or "P".

1. Figure out the lowest note of the interval.

2. The lowest note is the tonic of the major scale you will use.

3. Count up the major scale of the bottom note of the interval (on this page it is C) up the scale until you get to the top note of the interval counting scale degree numbers. Remember the number of the scale degree for the top note of the interval.

4. Is the quality U, M or P?

asc. M2

Key: G Major

Exercise

In the following exercises, you will use the steps from before to identify the following intervals in the key of G major. Remember you can count up the major scale just like you did for the harmonic intervals. Now, follow the same steps as for figuring out the harmonic intervals in your head. You are now in "easy major scale land" and qualities will only be "M" or "P".

1. Figure out the lowest note of the interval.

2. The lowest note is the tonic of the major scale you will use.

3. Count up the major scale of the bottom note of the interval (on this page it is G) up the scale until you get to the top note of the interval counting scale degree numbers. Remember the number of the scale degree for the top note of the interval.

4. Is the quality U, M or P?

asc. M2

More Ascending Melodic Intervals

You are no longer in "easy major scale land" and qualities can be m, M, P, A, and d. Uses p. 104-106 of *The Best Music Theory Book for Beginners 1.*

1. Figure out interval direction. p. 104.

2. Figure out the "some kind of" (use the **basic** musical alphabet, the lowest note is 1). p.105.

3. Which qualities could be used for the "some kind of" interval distance? p.106.

4. Figure out whole or half steps to know the quality of the interval (use the **full** musical alphabet). Compare with p.106.

5. Write the interval with direction, quality, and distance.

asc. M2

How to Think About Writing and Labeling Descending Intervals Reminder 1

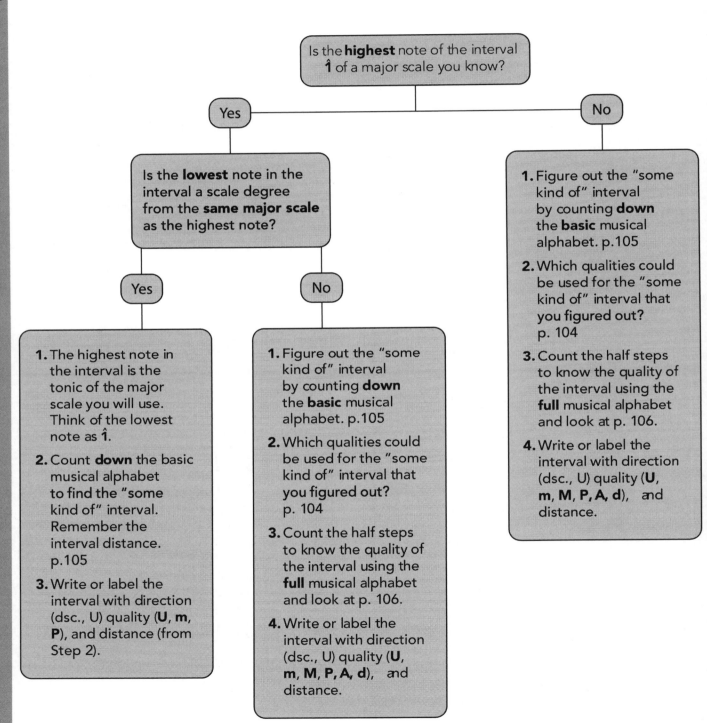

Is the **highest** note of the interval 1̂ of a major scale you know?

Yes

Is the **lowest** note in the interval a scale degree from the **same major scale** as the highest note?

Yes

1. The highest note in the interval is the tonic of the major scale you will use. Think of the lowest note as 1̂.
2. Count **down** the basic musical alphabet to find the "some kind of" interval. Remember the interval distance. p.105
3. Write or label the interval with direction (dsc., U) quality (**U, m, P**), and distance (from Step 2).

No

1. Figure out the "some kind of" interval by counting **down** the basic musical alphabet. p.105
2. Which qualities could be used for the "some kind of" interval that you figured out? p. 104
3. Count the half steps to know the quality of the interval using the **full** musical alphabet and look at p. 106.
4. Write or label the interval with direction (dsc., U) quality (**U, m, M, P, A, d**), and distance.

No

1. Figure out the "some kind of" interval by counting **down** the **basic** musical alphabet. p.105
2. Which qualities could be used for the "some kind of" interval that you figured out? p. 104
3. Count the half steps to know the quality of the interval using the **full** musical alphabet and look at p. 106.
4. Write or label the interval with direction (dsc., U) quality (**U, m, M, P, A, d**), and distance.

Interval Identification 4: Descending Intervals

Key: C Major

In the following exercises, you will use similar steps from the ascending and harmonic major scale intervals to identify the following descending intervals in the key of C major. Descending intervals for major scales are either m2, m3, m6, m7 or PU, P4, P5, P8. You are now in "easy major scale land: descending" and qualities will only be "m" or "P".

1. Figure out the highest note of the interval.

2. The highest note is the tonic of the major scale you will use.

3. Count backwards down the basic musical alphabet to find "some kind of" interval.

4. Is the quality m or P?

Tip: Remember that when you compare any descending note from any major scale to its root (for example, comparing any note of the C major scale to the note C) the quality of the interval will always be either minor or perfect. Perfect intervals: Unison (U), Fourth (4), Fifth (5), and Octave (8) minor intervals: Second (2), Third (3), Sixth (6), and Seventh (7).

Key: G Major

In the following exercises, you will use similar steps from the ascending and harmonic major scale intervals to identify the following descending intervals in the key of G major. Descending intervals for major scales are either m2, m3, m6, m7 or PU, P4, P5, P8. You are now in "easy major scale land: descending" and qualities will only be "m" or "P".

1. Figure out the highest note of the interval.

2. The highest note is the tonic of the major scale you will use.

3. Count backwards down the basic musical alphabet to find "some kind of" interval.

4. Is the quality m or P?

dsc. m2

Tip: Remember that when you compare any descending note from any major scale to its root (for example, comparing any note of the C major scale to the note C) the quality of the interval will always be either minor or perfect. Perfect intervals: Unison (U), Fourth (4), Fifth (5), and Octave (8) minor intervals: Second (2), Third (3), Sixth (6), and Seventh (7).

More Descending Melodic Intervals

You are no longer in "easy major scale land" and qualities can be m, M, P, A, and d. Uses p. 104-106 of *The Best Music Theory Book for Beginners 1*.

1. Figure out interval direction. p. 104.

2. Figure out the "some kind of" (use the **basic** musical alphabet, the highest note is 1). p. 105.

3. Which qualities could be used for the "some kind of" interval distance? p. 106.

4. Figure out whole or half steps to know the quality of the interval (use the **full** musical alphabet). Compare with p.106.

5. Write the interval with direction, quality, and distance.

dsc. M2

Write Harmonic Intervals: C & G

1. The already-written note is the tonic (1̂) of the major scale you will use.

2. Look at the interval label under the measure and remember the distance of the written interval label.

3. Count up the major scale of the already-written note, the tonic (1̂) of the interval up the scale until you get to the top note of the interval counting scale degree numbers to match the interval distance that is written under the measure.

4. Write in the missing note **above** or **next to** the written note to complete the interval including accidentals, ledger lines, and stems where needed. See stem rules on p. 108-109 of *The Best Music Theory Book for Beginners 1*.

5. For U and M2 intervals on ledger lines, you may need to extend the written ledger lines out to the left to write the second note of the interval. Below the staff, ledger lines on and above the second note are extended. Above the staff ledger lines on and below the second note are extended.

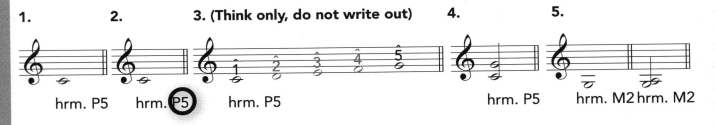

Whole Notes

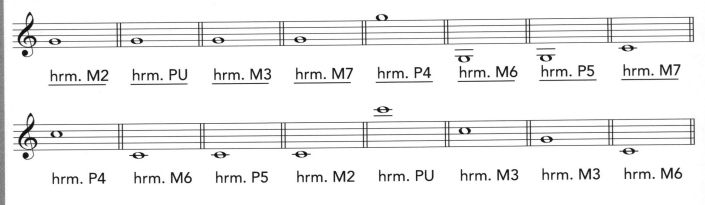

Half Notes

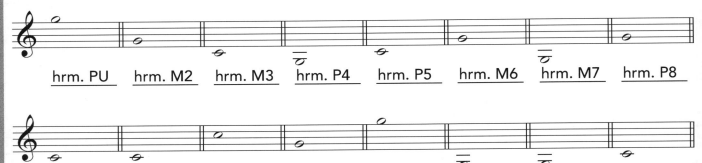

Write Ascending Intervals: C & G

1. The already-written note is the tonic (1̂) of the major scale you will use.

2. Look at the interval label under the measure and remember the distance of the written interval label.

3. Count up the major scale of the already-written note, the tonic (1̂) of the interval up the scale until you get to the top note of the interval counting scale degree numbers to match the interval distance that is written under the measure.

4. Write in the missing note **above and to the right** or **on the same line to the right** of the already-written note to complete the interval including accidentals, ledger lines and stems where needed. See stem rules on p. 108-109 of *The Best Music Theory Book for Beginners 1*.

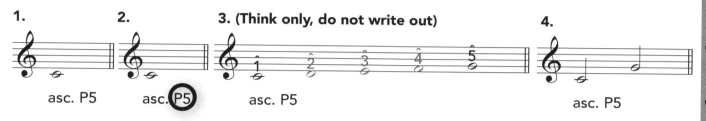

1.   **2.**   **3. (Think only, do not write out)**   **4.**

asc. P5   asc. P5   asc. P5   asc. P5

Whole Notes

PU   asc. M2   asc. M3   asc. P4   asc. P5   asc. M6   asc. M7   asc. P8

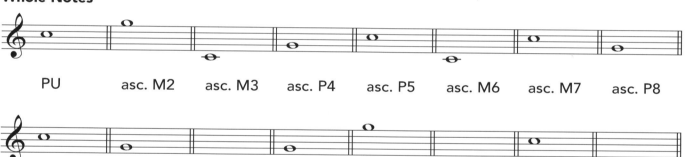

asc. P8   asc. M7   asc. M6   asc. P5   asc. P4   asc. M3   asc. M2   PU

Quarter Notes

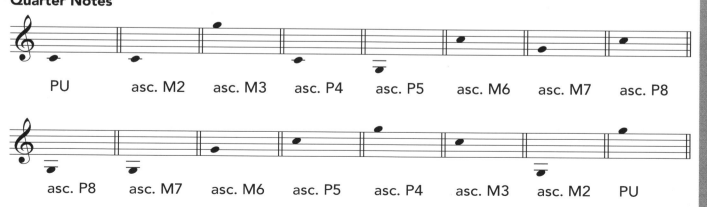

PU   asc. M2   asc. M3   asc. P4   asc. P5   asc. M6   asc. M7   asc. P8

asc. P8   asc. M7   asc. M6   asc. P5   asc. P4   asc. M3   asc. M2   PU

Write Descending Intervals: C & G

1. The highest note is the tonic (1̂) of the major scale you will use.

2. Look at the interval label under the measure and remember the distance of the written interval label.

3. Count down the basic musical alphabet from the already written note to get your "some kind of" interval distance to match the interval distance that is written under the measure.

4. Write in the missing note **below and to the right** or **on the same line to the right** of the already-written note to complete the interval including accidentals, ledger lines and stems where needed. See stem rules on p. 108-109 of *The Best Music Theory Book for Beginners 1*.

How to Think About Writing and Labeling Harmonic and Ascending Intervals Reminder 2

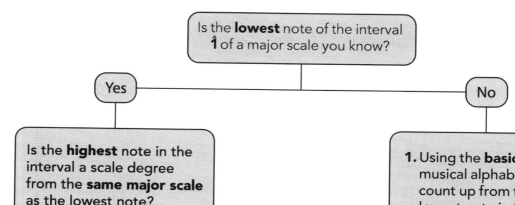

Is the **lowest** note of the interval 1̂ of a major scale you know?

Yes

No

Yes branch:

Is the **highest** note in the interval a scale degree from the **same major scale** as the lowest note?

Yes

No

Yes → Yes:

1. The lowest note in the interval is the tonic of the major scale you will use. Think of the lowest note as 1̂.

2. Count **up** the major scale of the lowest note up it's scale until you get to the highest (top) note of the interval counting scale degree numbers. Remember the scale degree number for the highest (top) note of the interval.

3. Write or label the interval with direction (asc., hrm., U) quality (**U, M, P**), and distance (scale degree number of the highest note).

Yes → No:

1. Using the **basic** musical alphabet count up from the lowest note in the interval to the highest note and figure out the "some kind of" interval. p.105

2. Which qualities could be used for the "some kind of" interval that you figured out? p. 104

3. Count the half steps to know the quality of the interval using the **full** musical alphabet and look at p. 106.

4. Write or label the interval with direction (asc. ,hrm. U) quality (**U, m, M, P, A, d**), and distance.

No branch:

1. Using the **basic** musical alphabet count up from the lowest note in the interval to the highest note and figure out the "some kind of" interval. p.105

2. Which qualities could be used for the "some kind of" interval that you figured out? p. 104

3. Count the half steps to know the quality of the interval using the **full** musical alphabet and look at p. 106.

4. Write or label the interval with direction (asc. ,hrm. U) quality (**U, m, M, P, A, d**), and distance.

How to Think About Writing and Labeling Descending Intervals Reminder 2

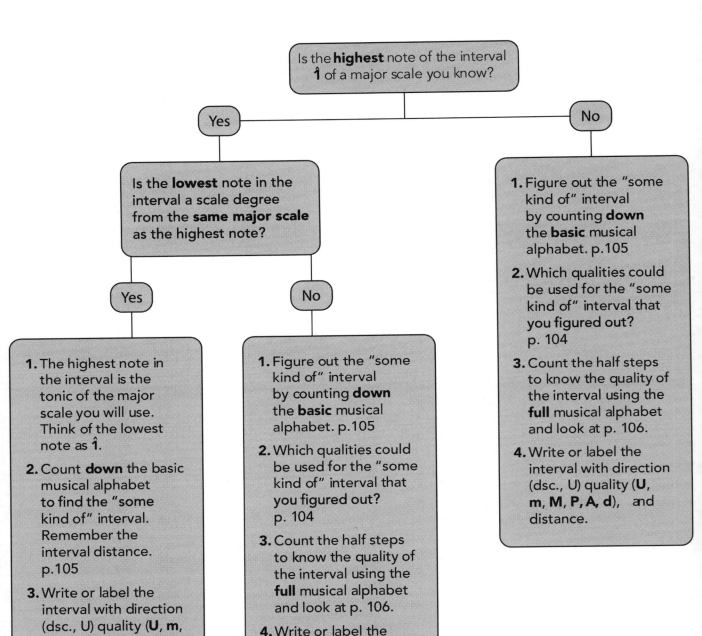

Is the highest note of the interval $\hat{1}$ of a major scale you know?

Yes

Is the lowest note in the interval a scale degree from the same major scale as the highest note?

Yes

1. The highest note in the interval is the tonic of the major scale you will use. Think of the lowest note as $\hat{1}$.
2. Count **down** the basic musical alphabet to find the "some kind of" interval. Remember the interval distance. p.105
3. Write or label the interval with direction (dsc., U) quality (**U, m, P**), and distance (from Step 2).

No

1. Figure out the "some kind of" interval by counting **down** the **basic** musical alphabet. p.105
2. Which qualities could be used for the "some kind of" interval that you figured out? p. 104
3. Count the half steps to know the quality of the interval using the **full** musical alphabet and look at p. 106.
4. Write or label the interval with direction (dsc., U) quality (**U, m, M, P, A, d**), and distance.

No

1. Figure out the "some kind of" interval by counting **down** the **basic** musical alphabet. p.105
2. Which qualities could be used for the "some kind of" interval that you figured out? p. 104
3. Count the half steps to know the quality of the interval using the **full** musical alphabet and look at p. 106.
4. Write or label the interval with direction (dsc., U) quality (**U, m, P, A, d**), and distance.

Writing More Simple Intervals

Harmonic

For tips and rules for writing simple intervals see p. 108-109 of *The Best Music Theory Book for Beginners 1*.

1. Complete the harmonic intervals by writing a note above/next to the note provided. Add a stem for half and quarter notes.

2. Think up the basic musical alphabet and figure out the "some kind of..." note would be to complete the interval name written below the staff.

3. Look at p. 106 of *The Best Music Theory Book for Beginners 1* to see how many half steps it will be to get to the quality of the interval name written below the staff.

4. Write in the second note with accidentals/stems above/next to the note to complete the interval.

Ascending

Complete the ascending intervals by writing a note to the right of the note provided. Add a stem for half and quarter notes.

1. Think up the basic musical alphabet and figure out the "some kind of..." note would be to complete the interval name written below the staff.

2. Look at p. 106 of *The Best Music Theory Book for Beginners 1* to see how many half steps it will be to get to the quality of the interval name written below the staff.

3. Write in the second note above and to the right/on the same line (PU only) as the already-written note with accidentals/stems where needed to complete the interval.

Whole Notes

Half Notes

Quarter Notes

Descending

Complete the descending intervals by writing a note to the right of the note provided. Add a stem for half and quarter notes.

1. Think down the basic musical alphabet and figure out the "some kind of..." note would be to complete the interval name written below the staff.

2. Look at p. 106 of *The Best Music Theory Book for Beginners 1* to see how many half steps it will be to get to the quality of the interval name written below the staff.

3. Write in the second note below and to the right/on the same line (PU only) as the already-written note with accidentals/stems where needed to complete the interval.

Whole Notes

dsc. m2   dsc. M7   dsc. M2   dsc. m7   dsc. m3   dsc. M6   dsc. M3   dsc. M6

dsc. P4   dsc. P5   dsc. A4   dsc. d5   dsc. M2   dsc. M6   dsc. P4   dsc. d5

Half Notes

dsc. P8   dsc. M7   dsc. m7   dsc. M6   dsc. m6   dsc. P5   dsc. d5   dsc. A4

dsc. P4   dsc. M3   dsc. m3   dsc. M2   dsc. m2   PU   dsc. M7   dsc. M2

Quarter Notes

dsc. m2   dsc. M2   dsc. m3   dsc. M3   dsc. P4   dsc. A4   dsc. d5   dsc. P5

dsc. m6   dsc. M6   dsc. m7   dsc. M7   dsc. P8   dsc. m2   dsc. P4   dsc. m6

Review: Pitch and Notes 4

- Melodic intervals
    - Ascending
    - Descending

- Harmonic intervals

- Major and minor intervals

- Interval quality 1
    - Major = M
    - minor = m
    - Perfect = P
    - Augmented = A
    - diminished = d
    - Unison intervals
    - Octave intervals

- Simple intervals: the full picture

- Interval quality 2
    - Introduction: consonance and dissonance
    - Perfect consonance
    - Imperfect consonance

- Interval direction
    - asc.
    - dsc.
    - hrm.

- Interval distance
    - Ascending intervals
    - Descending intervals
    - Harmonic intervals

- How to name simple intervals

- How to name intervals on leadsheets

- How to write simple intervals: melodic
    - How to write ascending simple intervals
    - How to write descending simple intervals
- How to write simple intervals: harmonic
    - Harmonic intervals: noteheads
    - Harmonic intervals: stems

New Words You Should Know

1. Ascending
2. Descending
3. Melodic
4. Harmonic
5. Interval
6. Perfect
7. Augmented
8. Diminished
9. Unison
10. Consonance
11. Dissonance
12. Perfect consonance
13. Imperfect consonance
14. Interval quality
15. Interval type
16. Interval distance

Memorize the number of half steps for m2 (1), M2 (2), m3 (3), and M3 (4). Look at p. 104 for all other interval distances.

Workbook
Harmony 1: Triads

Writing Triads

Naming Chord Tones

Write the letter name for each chord tone in the blank spaces.

G Major Chord Tones

Root:_____   Third:_____   Fifth:_____

E Minor Chord Tones

Root:_____   Third:_____   Fifth:_____

A Minor Chord Tones

Root:_____   Third:_____   Fifth:_____

C Major Chord Tones

Root:_____   Third:_____   Fifth:_____

Label the Root, Third, and Fifth

Write "Root" on the line next to the root of each chord. Write "Third" on the line next to the root of each chord. Write "Fifth" on the line next to the root of each chord.

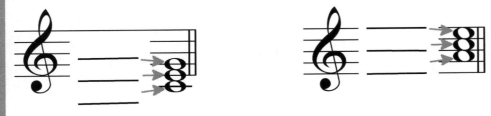

Write the Chord Symbol

Write the chord symbol in the blank.

Root: C   **Third: E**   **Fifth: G**   **Chord Symbol:** _____

Root: E   **Third: G**   **Fifth: B**   **Chord Symbol:** _____

Root: G   **Third: B**   **Fifth: D**   **Chord Symbol:** _____

Root: A   **Third: C**   **Fifth: E**   **Chord Symbol:** _____

Write the Triad Intervals

Write the interval quality and distance (PU, m2, M3, m3, M4, P4, P5) in the blanks.

Between the root and third of all major triads there is an interval of a _____

Between the third and fifth of all major triads there is an interval of a _____

Between the root and fifth of all major triads there is an interval of a _____

Between the root and third of all minor triads there is an interval of a _____

Between the third and fifth of all minor triads there is an interval of a _____

Between the root and fifth of all minor triads there is an interval of a _____

Label the Triad Intervals

Write the interval quality and distance (PU, m2, M3, m3, M4, P4, P5) next to the brackets.

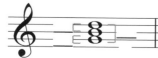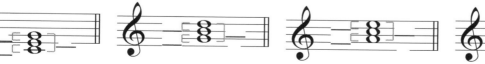

Writing Triads with Intervals 1

See p. 115 of *The Best Music Theory Book for Beginners 1* for a step-by-step walk-though for writing triads.

1. Is it a major triad? Write the third as a whole note, a M3 above the root.

2. Is it a minor triad? Write the third as a whole note, a m3 above the root.

3. Is it a major triad? Write the fifth as a whole note, a m3 above the third, which is the same as a P5 above the root.

4. Is it a minor triad? Write the fifth as a whole note, a M3 above the third, which is the same as a P5 above the root.

Tip: If the fifth is not a P5 above the root, you have made a mistake. Go back and try again.

Tip: When you write a triad, they should end up looking like a snowman!

Writing Triads with Accidentals 1

Write the triads for the chord symbol above each measure, starting on the note written below the staff. See p. 115 of *The Best Music Theory Book for Beginners 1* for a step-by-step walk-though for writing triads with accidentals. To review octave registers see p. 68 of *The Best Music Theory Book for Beginners 1*.

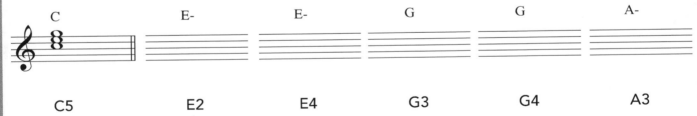

Writing Triads with Key Signatures

Write the triads for the chord symbol above each measure, starting on the note written below the staff. See p. 114 of *The Best Music Theory Book for Beginners 1* for a step-by-step walk-though for writing triads with key signatures.

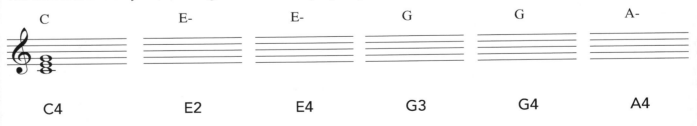

Writing Triads with Dots

See p. 116 of The Best Music Theory Book for Beginners 1 for a step-by-step walk-though for writing triads with dots.

Add Dots to the Triads

Add dots to each half note triad. Each notehead needs it's own dot.

Complete the Triad and Add Dots

Complete the triad using the provided note as the root of your triad. Add dots to complete your dotted half note triads, add stems, and accidentals if needed. Add courtesy accidentals if appropriate.

Writing Triads with Ties

See p. 116 of The Best Music Theory Book for Beginners 1 for a step-by-step walk-though for writing triads with ties.

Add the Ties to the Triads

Write the Second Triad and Add the Ties

Write the a G triad for the rhythmic value that will complete the measure in the blank beats of the staff. Add ties from the G triad in the previous measure to the one you have written.

Write the Chord Symbol 2

Write the chord symbol in the blank.

Key of C Major

Root: D   **Third: F**   **Fifth: A**   **Chord Symbol:** _____

Root: F   **Third: A**   **Fifth: C**   **Chord Symbol:** _____

Root: A   **Third: C**   **Fifth: E**   **Chord Symbol:** _____

Root: G   **Third: B**   **Fifth: D**   **Chord Symbol:** _____

Root: E   **Third: G**   **Fifth: B**   **Chord Symbol:** _____

Root: C   **Third: E**   **Fifth: G**   **Chord Symbol:** _____

Write The Major Triad Quality Formula

Fill in the blanks to complete The Major Triad Quality Formula.

Major _____ _____ **Major** _____ **Minor**

_____ **Minor Minor** _____ _____ _____

Major _____ _____ _____ _____ _____

Write Major Triad Quality Formula + Chord Symbols: C Major

1. Fill in the quality formula boxes with either "Major" or "Minor" for the chord quality.

2. Write the chord symbol in the chord symbols box for each chord in the key of C major.

Scale Degree	$\hat{1}$	$\hat{2}$	$\hat{3}$	$\hat{4}$	$\hat{5}$	$\hat{6}$	$\hat{7}$	$\hat{1}(\hat{8})$
Quality Formula	Major							
Chord Symbol	C							

Write the Chord Symbol 3

Key of G Major

Root: B   Third: D   Fifth: F♯   Chord Symbol: _____

Root: G   Third: B   Fifth: D   Chord Symbol: _____

Root: D   Third: F♯   Fifth: A   Chord Symbol: _____

Root: E   Third: G   Fifth: B   Chord Symbol: _____

Root: D   Third: F♯   Fifth: A   Chord Symbol: _____

Root: B   Third: D   Fifth: F♯   Chord Symbol: _____

Write The Major Triad Quality Formula: Review

Fill in the blanks to complete The Major Triad Quality Formula.

Major _____ _____ **Major** _____ **Minor**

_____ **Minor Minor** _____ _____ _____

Major _____ _____ _____ _____

Write Major Triad Quality Formula + Chord Symbols: G Major

1. Fill in the quality formula boxes with either "Major" or "Minor" for the chord quality.

2. Write the chord symbol in the chord symbols box for each chord in the key of G major.

Scale Degree	$\hat{1}$	$\hat{2}$	$\hat{3}$	$\hat{4}$	$\hat{5}$	$\hat{6}$	$\hat{7}$	$\hat{1}(\hat{8})$
Quality Formula	Major							
Chord Symbol	G							

Write the Triad Intervals 2: Reminder

Write the interval quality and distance (PU, m2, M3, m3, M4, P4, P5) in the blanks.

Between the root and third of all major triads there is an interval of a _____

Between the third and fifth of all major triads there is an interval of a _____

Between the root and fifth of all major triads there is an interval of a _____

Between the root and third of all minor triads there is an interval of a _____

Between the third and fifth of all minor triads there is an interval of a _____

Between the root and fifth of all minor triads there is an interval of a _____

Label the Triad Intervals and Chord Symbols

1. Write the interval quality and distance (PU, m2, M3, m3, M4, P4, P5) next to the brackets.

2. Write the chord symbol for each triad above the staff.

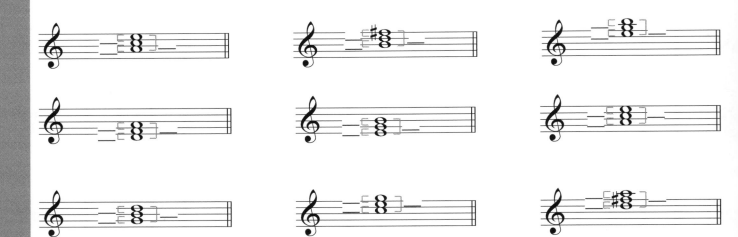

Writing Triads with Accidentals 2

See p. 119 of *The Best Music Theory Book for Beginners 1* for the walk-through for writing triads.

Write Triads with Whole Notes

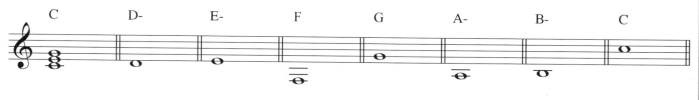

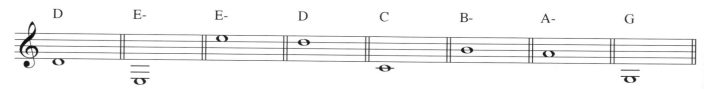

Write Triads with Half Notes (Write the noteheads, then add the stem)

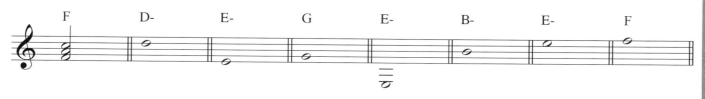

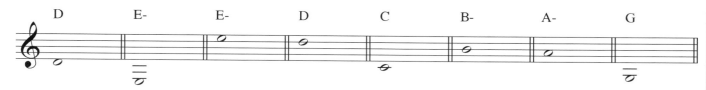

Write Triads with Quarter Notes (Write the noteheads, then add the stem)

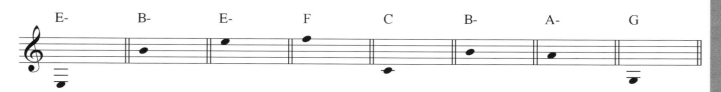

Writing Triads In the Key of G Major

Write all triads as if you are in the key of G major. Watch out for the F chord in the second line! You will need a natural accidental for the F.

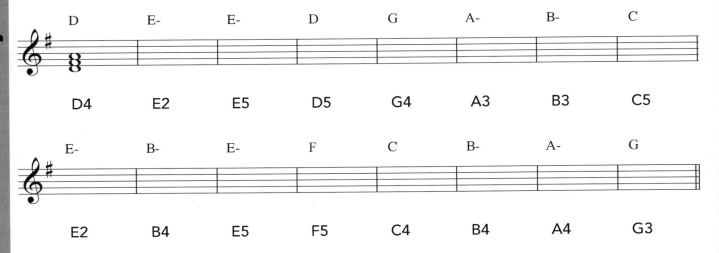

Triad Identification

Write the chord symbol for the written triad above the measure for each triad.

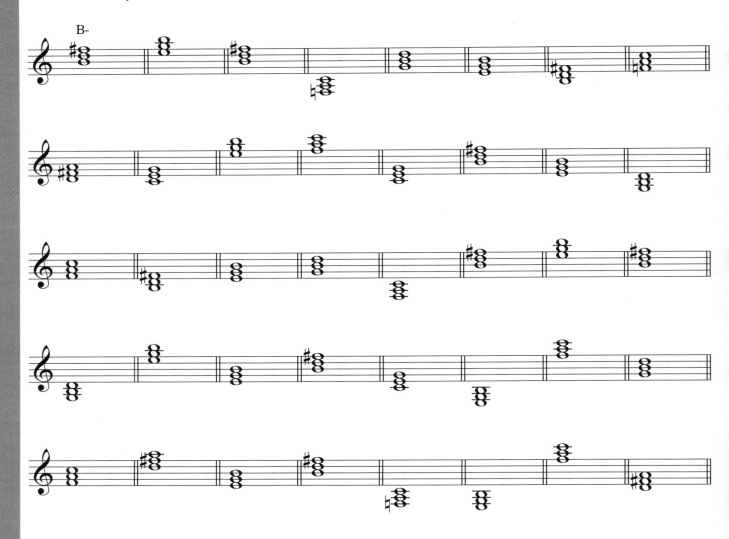

Writing Roman Numerals: Major Scales and Keys

In the following exercises, you will practice writing and identifying roman numerals in the keys of C and G.

C Major Write the Roman Numerals Below the Staff

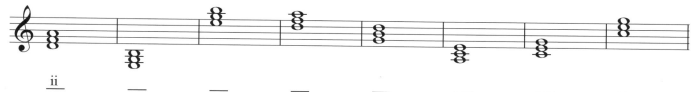

ii

G Major Write the Roman Numerals Below the Staff

Remember that in the G major example, every time you see the note "F," it is actually an F#.

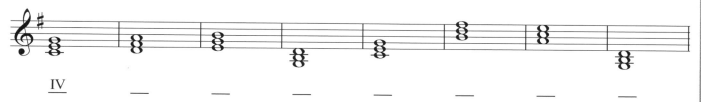

IV

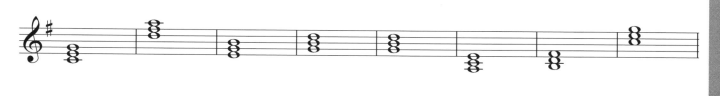

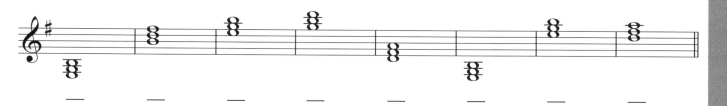

G Major Write the Triads for the Roman Numerals

The answer key for this exercise shows only one particular triad. As long as you have the right chord root and quality, it counts as a correct answer. For example, if you write an A- triad starting on A4, but the answer key has an A - triad starting on A3, it is still a correct answer.

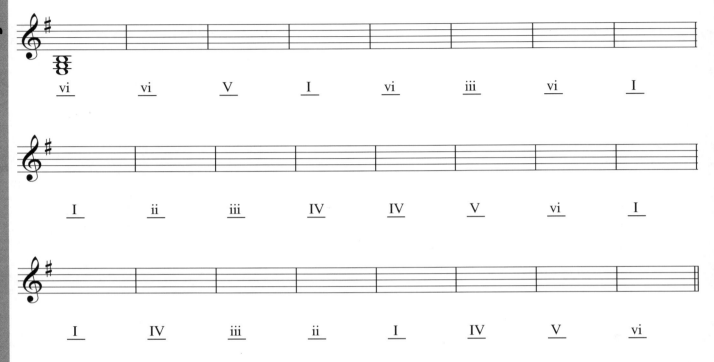

vi   vi   V   I   vi   iii   vi   I

I   ii   iii   IV   IV   V   vi   I

I   IV   iii   ii   I   IV   V   vi

C Major Write the Triads for the Roman Numerals

The answer key for this exercise shows only one particular triad. As long as you have the right chord root and quality, it counts as a correct answer. When the same RN is repeated, challenge yourself to write it in a different octave as the answer you gave for that RN earlier in the exercise.

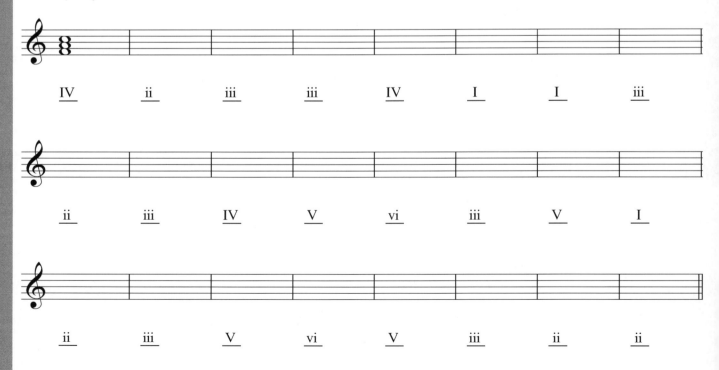

IV   ii   iii   iii   IV   I   I   iii

ii   iii   IV   V   vi   iii   V   I

ii   iii   V   vi   V   iii   ii   ii

Writing Major Scales Harmonized to the Fifth

See p. 120 of *The Best Music Theory Book for Beginners 1* for a full walk-through on harmonizing major scales.

With Accidentals

C Major Scale Harmonized to the Fifth

Start on the provided note and harmonize the C major scale to the fifth (write a triad for each scale degree) to $\hat{6}$. Add accidentals when needed. Add roman numerals below each chord and chord symbols above each chord. Start on the note provided.

G Major Scale Harmonized to the Fifth

Start on the provided note and harmonize the G major scale to the fifth to $\hat{6}$. Add accidentals when needed. Add roman numerals below each chord and chord symbols above each chord. Start on the note provided.

With Key Signatures

C Major Scale Harmonized to the Fifth

Start on the provided note and harmonize the C major scale to the fifth with a key signature to $\hat{6}$. Add roman numerals below each chord and chord symbols above each chord. Start on the note provided.

G Major Scale Harmonized to the Fifth

Start on the provided note and harmonize the G major scale to the fifth with a key signature to $\hat{6}$. Add roman numerals below each chord and chord symbols above each chord. Start on the note provided.

Natural Minor Chords

Write The Minor Triad Quality Formula

Fill in the blanks to complete The Major Triad Quality Formula.

Minor Skip _____ _____ **Minor** _____ **Major**

_____ **Skip Major** _____ _____ _____ _____

_____ **Skip** _____ _____ _____ _____ _____

Connect the Chords to the Scales

Write a line connecting each chord to the harmonized scales that it can be found in. C is already done as an example.

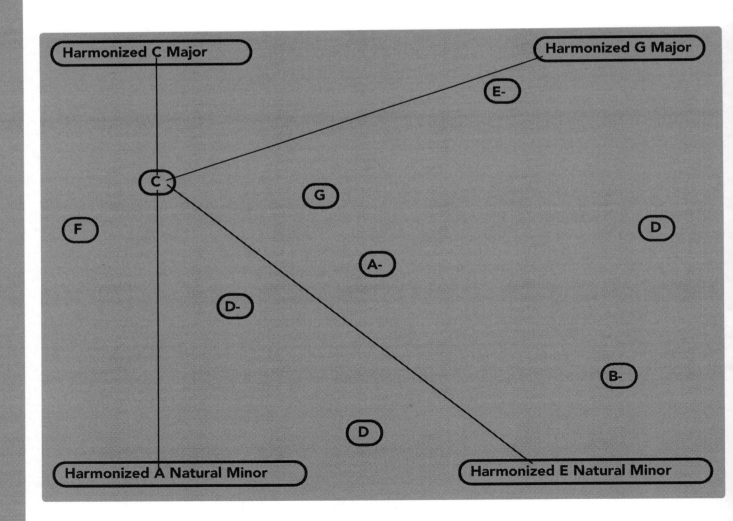

Writing Roman Numerals: Natural Minor Scales and Keys

In the following exercises, you will practice writing and identifying roman numerals in the keys of A and E minor.

A Minor Write the Roman Numerals Below the Staff

iv _____ _____ _____ _____ _____ _____ _____

_____ _____ _____ _____ _____ _____ _____ _____

_____ _____ _____ _____ _____ _____ _____ _____

E Minor Write the Roman Numerals Below the Staff

Remember that in the E minor example, every time you see the note "F," it is actually an F#.

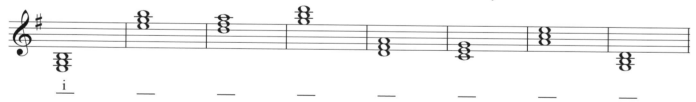

i _____ _____ _____ _____ _____ _____ _____

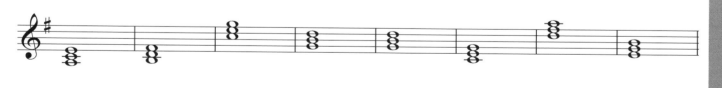

_____ _____ _____ _____ _____ _____ _____ _____

_____ _____ _____ _____ _____ _____ _____ _____

Harmony 1: Triads

E Minor Write the Triads for the Roman Numerals

The answer key for this exercise shows only one particular triad. As long as you have the right chord root and quality, it counts as a correct answer. For example, if you write an A- triad starting on A4, but the answer key has an A - triad starting on A3, it is still a correct answer.

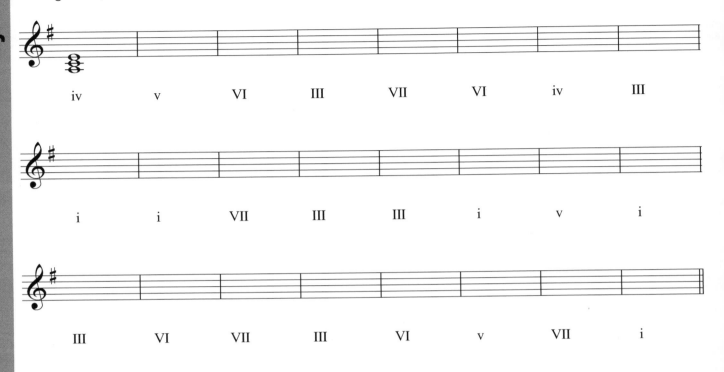

| | iv | v | VI | III | VII | VI | iv | III |

| | i | i | VII | III | III | i | v | i |

| | III | VI | VII | III | VI | v | VII | i |

A Minor Write the Triads for the Roman Numerals

The answer key for this exercise shows only one particular triad. As long as you have the right chord root and quality, it counts as a correct answer. When the same RN is repeated, challenge yourself to write it in a different octave as the answer you gave for that RN earlier in the exercise.

| | III | iv | v | v | v | iv | v | iv |

| | III | VII | III | VII | iv | v | i | VII |

| | VI | iv | v | III | VII | i | VI | VI |

Writing Natural Minor Scales Harmonized to the Fifth

See p. 124-125 of *The Best Music Theory Book for Beginners 1* for a full walk-through on harmonizing natural minor scales.

With Accidentals

A Natural Minor Scale Harmonized to the Fifth

Start on the provided note and harmonize the A natural minor scale to the fifth, skipping $\hat{2}$. Add accidentals when needed. Add roman numerals below each chord and chord symbols above each chord. Start on the note provided.

E Natural Minor Scale Harmonized to the Fifth

Start on the provided note and harmonize the E natural minor scale to the fifth, skipping $\hat{2}$. Add accidentals when needed. Add roman numerals below each chord and chord symbols above each chord. Start on the note provided.

With Key Signatures

A Natural Minor Scale Harmonized to the Fifth

Start on the provided note and harmonize the A natural minor scale to the fifth **with a key signature**, skipping $\hat{2}$. Add roman numerals below each chord and chord symbols above each chord. Start on the note provided.

E Natural Minor Scale Harmonized to the Fifth

Start on the provided note and harmonize the E natural minor scale to the fifth **with a key signature**, skipping $\hat{2}$. Add roman numerals below each chord and chord symbols above each chord. Start on the note provided.

More Triad Identification

1. Write a chord symbol to represent the triad. Chord symbols typically are shown above the staff, for this exercise we are doing it a little differently so you can see the RN and the chord symbol closer to each other.

2. Write a roman numeral to show how the triad relates to the key.

C Major

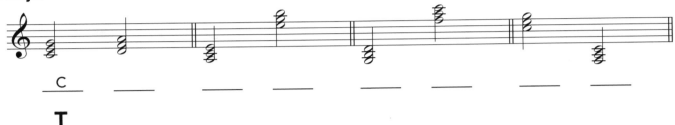

___C___   _____   _____   _____   _____   _____   _____

___I___   _____   _____   _____   _____   _____   _____

A Minor

___A-___   _____   _____   _____   _____   _____   _____

___i___   _____   _____   _____   _____   _____   _____

G Major

___G___   _____   _____   _____   _____   _____   _____

___I___   _____   _____   _____   _____   _____   _____

E Minor

___E-___   _____   _____   _____   _____   _____   _____

___i___   _____   _____   _____   _____   _____   _____

Review: Harmony 1

- Harmony
- What is a chord?
  - Intervals
  - Dyads
- Triads
- Chord tones
  - Root
  - Third
  - Fifth
- Major vs. minor triads
- How to name a chord
  - Root note
  - Quality
- How to understand triads: intervals
- How to write triads
  - Stem rules
  - How to write triads with accidentals
  - How to write triads with key signatures
- Triads: the major scale harmonized to the fifth
- New triads
- Roman numerals
- How to write a harmonized major scale to the fifth
  - How to write a harmonized major scale to the fifth with accidentals
  - How to write a harmonized major scale to the fifth with a key signature
- Triads: the natural minor scale harmonized to the fifth
- How to write a natural minor scale harmonized to the fifth
  - How to write a natural minor scale harmonized to the fifth with accidentals
  - How to write a natural minor scale harmonized to the fifth with a key signature
- How to identify triads

New Words You Should Know

1. Harmony
2. Chord
3. Dyad
4. Triad
5. Chord tone
6. Root
7. Third
8. Fifth
9. Chord quality
10. Harmonized
11. Roman numerals

Workbook
Analysis 1: Degrees and Numerals

Key Identification 1

Key Signature Identification

Write in the key symbol for each key signature. There is one major and one minor key that fits with each key signature.

No Accidentals = ___ / ___-

One Sharp = ___ / ___-

Chords

Does the chord progression show a major key or a minor key? Circle the answer for each progression.

C   A-   F   G

Major   Minor

C   G   A-   F

Major   Minor

A-   F   C   G

Major   Minor

E-   A-   B-   E-

Major   Minor

Melody

Is it Major or Minor?

1. Write the scale degrees as if the music is in the major key associated with the key signature.

2. Write the scale degrees as if the music is in the minor key associated with the key signature.

3. Based on the Common Notes + which beats they land on, which is more likely, major or minor? Circle the correct answer.

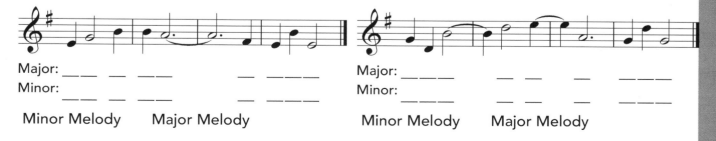

Major: ___ ___ ___ ___ ___ ___   Major: ___ ___ ___ ___ ___ ___

Minor: ___ ___ ___ ___ ___ ___   Minor: ___ ___ ___ ___ ___ ___

Minor Melody   Major Melody   Minor Melody   Major Melody

Review: How to Identify the Key of a Leadsheet: Final Decision

To make a final decision on what key a written piece of music is in ask yourself the following questions and think about the information below.

1. Key Signature: Major and Minor Keys

- There are 4 possible keys: C, G, A-, E-.
- What are the two possible keys that this song could be in?
- Looking at the key signature, which major key and which minor key (they will always be relative major and minor) could you use? (C/A- or G/E-)

2. Chords: Chords and Chord Progressions

- Do the chords show a Common Chord Progression?
- Do all the chords come from the harmonized scale that is the same name as the key? Example: if there are chords from a harmonized G major scale and you think the key is A-, go back to step 1: Key Signature because you got the key signature wrong.
- What are the first and last chords?
- Which chords are used the most?
- There can be minor chords in a major key and major chords in a minor key.
- If there are no or very few minor chords in the song, the key is probably major.
- If there are no or very few major chords in the song, the key is probably minor.
- Are the chords showing a major key or a minor key?

3. Melody: Common Notes and Strong Beats

- Are there major or minor Common Notes or $\hat{1}$ from one of the two possible keys on strongest and strong beats in the first few and last few measures?
- Think of the scale degrees in terms of the major key. Which scale degrees fall on the strongest and strong beats of the first few and last few measures?
- Think of the scale degrees in terms of the major key. Which scale degrees fall on the strongest and strong beats of the first few and last few measures?
- Are the melody and common notes showing a major key or a minor key?

Key of the Song =

Chords/Progression = Major +	Common Notes = Major =	Major Key!
Chords/Progression = Can't Tell +	Common Notes = Major =	Major Key!
Chords/Progression = Minor +	Common Notes = Minor =	Minor Key!
Chords/Progression = Can't Tell +	Common Notes = Minor =	Minor Key!

Key Identification 2

For a full walk-through of key identification see p. 132 of *The Best Music Theory Book for Beginners 1*.

Exercise 1

Identify the key of this song. Write the key in the box below the first measure followed by a colon. Example: A- :

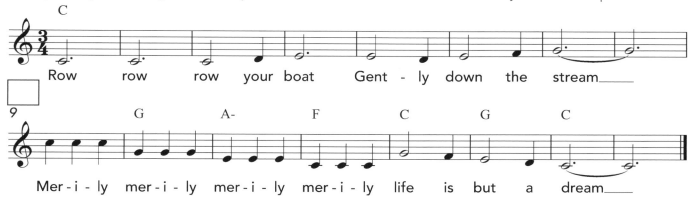

Exercise 2

Identify the key of this song. Write the key in the box below the first measure followed by a colon. Example: A- :

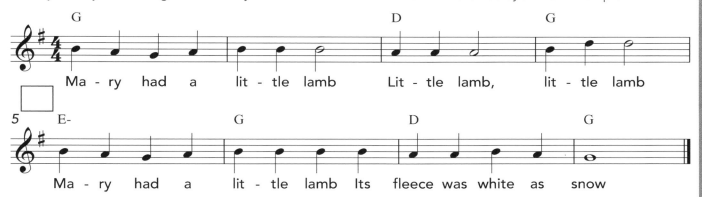

Exercise 3

Identify the key of this song. Write the key in the box below the first measure followed by a colon. Example: A- :. This is not the full song, so look to the first few measures and chords to figure out the key.

Exercise 4

Identify the key of this song. Write the key in the box below the first measure followed by a colon. Example: A- :

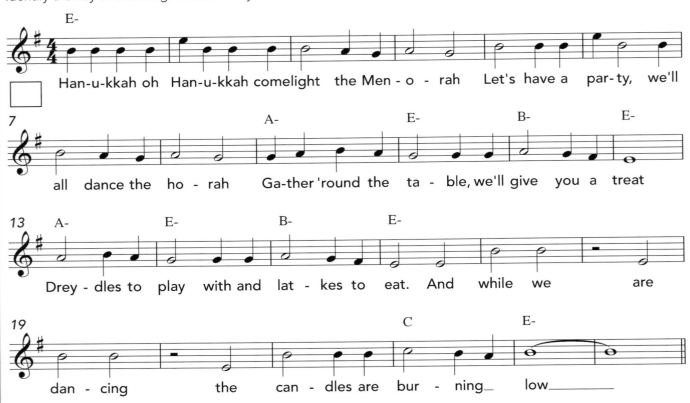

Exercise 5

Identify the key of this song. Write the key in the box below the first measure followed by a colon. Example: A- :

Scale Degree Analysis

Write the key, then a full scale degree analysis of each exercise. p. 133 of *The Best Music Theory Book for Beginners 1*

Exercise 1

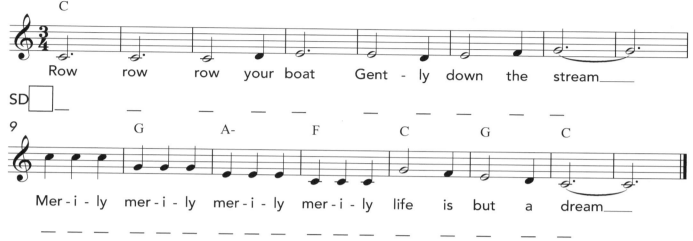

Exercise 2

Exercise 3

Exercise 4

Roman Numeral Analysis

For the following exercises, write in the key in the box, then perform a roman numeral analysis, also called a "harmonic analysis". For a full walk-through, see p. 134 of *The Best Music Theory Book for Beginners 1*.

Exercise 1

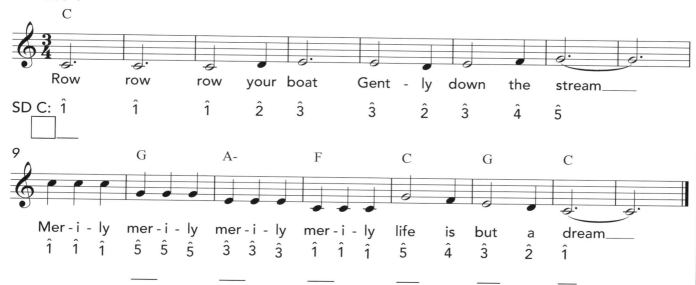

Exercise 2

Exercise 3

Exercise 4

Exercise 5

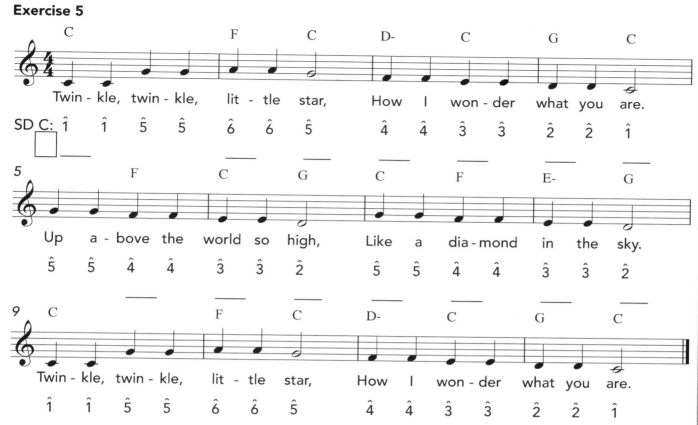

Review: Analysis 1

- How to analyze lead sheets
- How to read leadsheets
    Chords
    Melody
    Lyrics
- 3 steps to identify a leadsheet or song
    Key signature
    Chords
    Common notes
- How to identify the key of a leadsheet: key signature
- How to identify the key of a leadsheet: chords
- How to identify the key of a leadsheet: common notes
- How to identify the key of a leadsheet: final decision
- How to write an analysis 1
    How to write the key of a piece of music
    How to write a scale degree analysis
    How to write a roman numeral analysis

What's Next?

1. Complete your Level 1 Theory workbook!
2. Take your final Theory Level 1 quiz...
3. Get your Level 1 Music Theory Certificate! (Snap a selfie with it + tag @ bestmusiccoach!!)
4. Analyze 5-10 Level 1: Leadsheet songs from bestsheetmusic.com

Level 2

In the next book "*The Music Theory Book for Beginners: 2*" you will learn so much more cool and applicable theory so you can understand even more music and take your playing, singing, writing, composing or music appreciation to the next level!

We Want to Hear From You!

Let us know what you think about this book, how we can make this book better for you, and what else you would like to see from Best Music Coach!

support@bestmusiccoach.com

www.bestmusiccoach.com

facebook.com/bestmusiccoach

youtube.com/bestmusiccoach

twitter.com/bestmusiccoach

instagram.com/bestmusiccoach

Acknowledgments

Eli's Acknowledgments

Thank you to all those who have played and continue to play fundamental roles in my journey as a musician and as a human being. To my family and friends, music teachers and mentors from my beginnings all the way through my graduation from Berklee to today - I would not be who I am without you. I am beyond grateful for you and for the fact that there are too many of you to list.

Mom, Dad, Max, and Sammy - thank you for being there since day one.

-        Eli Slavkin

Dan's Acknowledgments

Thank you Jasara for your radical support.

Sources:

Many of the rules for engraving in this book can be traced directly to *Behind Bars: The Definitive Guide to Music Notation* - Elaine Gould.
ISBN: 978-0571514564